Jack Crawford, Leigh Hadley Irvine

The Poet Scout

a Book of Song and Story

Jack Crawford, Leigh Hadley Irvine

The Poet Scout
a Book of Song and Story

ISBN/EAN: 9783743329294

Manufactured in Europe, USA, Canada, Australia, Japa

Cover: Foto ©Thomas Meinert / pixelio.de

Manufactured and distributed by brebook publishing software (www.brebook.com)

Jack Crawford, Leigh Hadley Irvine

The Poet Scout

THE

POET SCOUT.

A BOOK OF SONG AND STORY.

BY

CAPTAIN JACK CRAWFORD,

(Late Chief of Scouts, U. S. Army.)

FUNK & WAGNALLS:

NEW YORK: 1886.   LONDON:

10–12 DEY STREET.   44 FLEET STREET.

PREFACE.

In the publication of the sketches and poems in the following pages I have no thought of grasping literary or poetical distinction. They are the crude, unpolished offspring of my idle hours—wandering thoughts which came to me on the lonely trail and in the bivouac and camp. They were written with no studied effort, but are the spontaneous bubblings from a heart whose springs of poesy and poetic thought were opened by the hand of Nature amid her roughest scenes. In the selections herein produced many past incidents of an adventurous life have reproduced themselves on the memory, and taken the shape of verse. That they are crude and rough and lack the polished finish of the droppings from more gifted pens, I freely admit, and I would therefore beg the critics to spare them.

I have never figured as a hero of fiction or dime novels, and have refused to allow my name to be used in connection with that kind of literature ; hence I come before you with my " Poet Scout" in a measure unheralded. I had a Christian mother, my earliest recollection of whom was kneeling at her side, praying God to save a wayward father and husband. That mother taught me to speak the truth when a child, and I have tried to follow her early teachings in that respect. It would require a much larger book than this to tell the story of my life and the sufferings of one of God's good angels—my mother. To her I owe everything—truth, honor, sobriety, and even my very life. Her spirit seems to linger near me always ; she has been my guardian angel. In the camp, the cabin, the field, and the hospital, on the lonely trail, hundreds of miles from civilization, in the pine-clad hills and lonely cañons, I have heard in the moaning night winds and in the murmuring streamlets

> The voice of my angel mother
> Whispering soft and low.

And these sacred thoughts have made me forget at times that there was danger in my pathway. Nor will I ever forget

> The day that we parted, mother and I,
>   Never on earth to meet again ;
> She to a happier home on high,
>   I a poor wanderer over the plain.

That day was perhaps the greatest epoch in my life. Kneeling by her bedside, with one hand clasped in mine, the other resting upon my head, she whispered : " My boy, you know your mother loves you. Will you give me a promise, that I may take it up to heaven ?" " Yes, yes, mother ; I will promise you anything." "Johnny, my son, I am dying," said she ; " promise me you will never drink intoxicants, and then it will not be so hard to leave this world." Dear reader, need I tell you that I promised " Yes ;" and whenever I am asked to drink, that scene comes up before me, and I am safe.

With these few words I launch my little craft upon the great sea of literature, trusting that it may sail smoothly and weather every gale.

JOHN WALLACE CRAWFORD.

CONTENTS.

BIOGRAPHICAL SKETCH.

BY LEIGH IRVINE.

A ruddy drop of manly blood
The surging sea outweighs.—EMERSON.

SINCE the earliest eras of myth and fable all races have paid homage to
heroism. There is in the constitution of man a tendency to hero-worship, and
power always commands a certain reverence. We never tire of believing in the
resources of Nature and in the hidden possibilities of man ; hence we are ever
encouraged to learn of any unusual feats of our fellow-men. Revelations
of virtue, courage, skill, and remarkable powers of endurance are always received
with wonder and pleasure, for they help to build in the mind a hope. They lead
us to believe that "what man has done man can do," and to trust in the benefi-
cence of Nature. Almost any stories of the exploits of men are interesting if
true, provided they give us a new insight into the history of the human mind.
However humble the actor or rugged the scene in which he is depicted, it is
in a certain sense MAN acting and living under the varied circumstances of the
age and country in which the special agent is stationed.

It is wonderful what a fascination is inwoven with stories of life in the far
West! Tales of frontier times charm us and hold our attention even as did the
legends and Arabian fictions of boyhood days. The very landscapes in the
country of the setting sun are vast and awe-inspiring, and they seem to com-
municate to man somewhat of their own broad proportions. It has been the
universal conclusion of careful observers that men who go from old settle-
ments in the East to the mining regions or plains of the West become broad-
minded, good-natured, and liberal if there were any such tendencies in their
characters. The Western man is noticeable for his frankness and generosity ;
and even though his manner be strikingly unconventional there is seldom a
question that his motive has origin in good-fellowship. Who that has ever
known a genuine frontiersman of '49 can forget his open hospitality? In

his presence one feels that all is clear as the diamond mornings of June. There is no need of condescension or apology for anything. The rugged child of the mountains stands firmly on his feet, as much as to say that all men exist by inalienable right. Hypocrisy, greed, stinginess, and all petty quibbling are forgotten. His smallest measure of value for years was four or five times what we pay for a loaf of bread or a glass of beer, and his "dust" is divided with a generosity that puts to shame the liberality we have known in other lands. I have never looked upon these Atlantean-shouldered giants of the new West without feeling in a certain sense that they grew thus rich in physical powers and cleverness from contemplating the bounty of Nature, the plentifulness of landscape, the wastes of mountains and plains. A certain grandeur attaches even to the arched sky and silent stars when beheld from high mountains or viewed from the depths of grand cañons walled with sublime rocks and mountains crowned with peaks of perennial snow. Buckle's theory that the vast mountains of Asia make the inhabitants superstitious and cowardly may be true; but the "Rockies" and Sierras of the American continent seem to inspire men with courage and renewed confidence in the strength of manhood. The same statement is true of the boundless plains of the West. The cow-boy stands as a perpetual contradiction to any philosophy which teaches that the vastness of Nature makes man believe in his own insignificance. He has never had any misgivings as to his right to life, liberty, and happiness after his own fashion.

It is comparatively seldom that one meets a real hero in the West, one entitled in any high and philosophic sense to be classed with men of extraordinary powers. There are many to whom is due the credit of personal intrepidity, for their valor goes without question. They are bold in danger and fearless in the presence of mortal foes. Like the old Spartan gladiators, who were willing to face man or beast in the arena of bloody combat, they do not fear sanguinary conflicts, and their courage remains unabated to the end. But physical valor alone is not the full measure of heroism. Life is more than a series of conflicts, and its true rewards do not rest purely on a physical basis. The greatest man, the most heroic man, must lead a life which spans a wider field than animal endurance or good-fellowship. The true hero does not forget that man has an intellectual and a moral side in his nature. The old heroes were supposed to be children of the gods, and the gods were not of the flesh, but of the mind or spirit. "The gods of fable are the shining moments of great men." Nothing is truer than that the mind is in a high degree the measure of the man. The highest unit is, therefore, one that deals not alone with acts of physical bravery, but with the mental life as well.

Men who have the courage to think for themselves are rare, and those whose thoughts are morally pure and clear with the light of truth are rarer still. It is one of the most difficult of tasks to think, and next to this is to give a thought skilful expression, the clothing of clear language. Then how are we to estimate a man who, amid the conflicts of Indian warfare and the surroundings of miners' camps, not only acquired a fair education, but learned to commune with Nature and long for the inspiration of her divine afflatus? Has he not interesting elements in his mental constitution, and such a faithfulness to the true ideals of life as to attract admiration? This higher heroism demands a finer feeling and rarer powers than the simple conquests due to bone, muscle, dapper exploits, and animal courage. If we find in one individual the combined beauties of an active mind, a brave spirit and great physical courage, he becomes exceedingly interesting. We long to know him, to see and feel his personality. Such a man is Captain J. W. Crawford, familiarly known as "Captain Jack." His ambition for self culture never flagged for a moment, whether on the soldier's march or by the trapper's lonely fireside.

Captain Crawford's character is unique, and his life is full of incident. He is a rare example of a brave frontiersman, with a fine mind and a tender heart. Border life seems to have made him gentle rather than to have hardened him, while the grandeur of nature moved him to write poetry. At first glance it seems that there is an incompatibility between an Indian scout and a poet, and many persons are loath to believe that a man whose life was spent in frontier pursuits and Indian warfare can write readable poetry. It was, however, the theory of Macaulay that poets thrived in early ages, and that civilization is necessarily destructive of bards. If this is true, there is something worthy of consideration in the fact that the great West more nearly fulfils the conditions named by Macaulay as being favorable to the production of poetry than any other part of the American continent. The primeval forests, the "wild torrents fiercely glad," and the wealth of vast wastes in nature combine to give to minds of poetic tendencies that fulness of imagination and love of the beautiful which the complexities of civilization in crowded cities render in a manner impossible. If there is any music in a man's soul, it will find expression amid the primal scenes of the lands where Captain Crawford spent many years of his life, hearing voices in the air " as of nymphs that haunt the mountain summits and the river founts, and the moist, grassy meadows." The power of feeling the impressions made by Nature on the mind and heart is one of the first requisites of the poet. A broad, good-hearted man, whose life leads in rugged paths, learns to know the value of friendship and to recognize true manhood at a glance. In the same surroundings he becomes an expert at detecting hypocrisy. Many of the poet scout's ballads celebrate the homely virtues of every-day life, or remove from deceit its hollow mask. His vocabulary abounds in expressions which glorify the graces of simple manhood, and for this reason even his rudest lines of dialect imitation have a beauty and freshness that are admirable. Such verses readily become popular with the masses, and nothing is more frequent than to hear some of his lines familiarly quoted in certain parts of the West where they have been published. The poem entitled " Rattlin' Joe's Prayer " has long been a favorite selection with many elocutionists and public readers. Though it is one of the roughest poems he has written, and though it abounds in slang, it is a perfect picture of the phase of life with which it deals. Where is a verse that gives a more satisfactory glimpse into the rude life of a miner than the following?

> "I'm lost on the rules o' yer game, but I'll ax
> Fur a seat fur him back o' yer throne.
> And I'll bet my whole stack that the boy'll behave,
> If yer angels jist lets him alone."

A striking example from a poem which abounds in the lessons of justice, and which contains throughout a commendable philosophy, is found in the first verse of "Hood's Children," a poem first read at a G. A. R. entertainment for their benefit in San Francisco. The sentence is as follows:

> "Dear comrades and friends in the golden land,
> You may say I'm rough, you may call me wild,
> But I've got a heart and a willing hand
> To feel and to work for a soldier's child."

A verse from a little poem suggested by a New York newsboy's contribution to the Grant monument fund is also in point:

> "And, boys, who knows, though his dad is dead,
> This peer of your snob galoots
> May be carving his way to the nation's head,
> Selling papers and blacking boots."

No one has ever claimed that any of Captain Crawford's poetry is comparable to the transcendental musings of an Emerson or the classic songs of Tennyson or Holmes; but there is in them a simple melody and a sentiment ever dear to the masses of mankind. Burns and Moore wrote on themes of no wider scope than those embraced within the catalogue of subjects essayed by Captain Crawford. In his most unfinished songs there is often a vigor, freshness, and originality which hold the attention, even if they do violence to the rhetoric of the reader. As a writer in the New York *Herald* a few years ago said: "If his verses had no other merit, they might be commended to the other Western dialect poets as a genuine fount of raw material for them to draw from." The collection is a kind of kaleidoscope, into which each reader must look for himself and then judge whether the colors and arrangement of colors are good. It must never be forgotten that every line he ever wrote was produced under the disadvantages of a fragmentary education, gained during the storms and conflicts of adult life. Considering him as a backwoodsman, a man without the advantages of culture, whose mature life has been passed mainly upon the cheerless plains, in contest with savages and in the society of the Western barrack-room and the trapper's hut, he is a wonderful personage. Under different training the rough diamond of his nature would have sparkled in the light of the literary world.

While considering this phase of the man's life, it may be of interest to many persons to know something of his methods in writing. An anonymous writer in the *Grand Army Magazine* for March, 1883, says that he is at times a very rapid composer. The following incident is cited:

"I asked Jack to return to town with me and talk over old times. On our arrival at Chloride, and after the usual questions as to old comrades had been answered, I said:

"'Well, Jack, I understand you have published a book of your poetry. I'll tell you what I wish you would do for me as a favor: just prove to these friends of mine around here that you can write. They are not skeptical, yet I would like to show them what you can do, and how quick you can do it.'

"Jack replied: 'All right; give me a subject, and I'll write you a verse or two.'

"Some one of our friends replied: 'Give us a song, with a regular miner's chorus.'

"I won't swear to it, but this I will say, as I had no watch, that in fifteen minutes Jack handed me a poem."

The writer then describes how the performance astonished the company. The following two verses from that extemporaneous effort may serve to give the reader some sort of insight into the man and his methods:

> " Hear the music of the hammer,
>   As it bounds from rock and drill;
> See the ore piled near the windlass
>   As it glistens on the hill;
> Hear the 'giant' cannonading,
>   Throwing out its precious load,
> And the merry song at evening
>   In the miner's log abode.
>
> " There's a vein of love and pathos
>   In each hardy miner's breast,
> And the thoughts of home and lov'd ones,
>   As he lays him down to rest,
> Are as sweet to him—though humble—
>   As the king upon his throne,
> For the miner's heart oft lingers
>   With the loving ones at home."

Being introduced to a beautiful young lady in 1875 named Franke Bailey, she asked Captain Jack to write an acrostic on her name, and in less than two minutes he handed her the following:

"Fairest flower, didst ever mortal eyes
Regard thee with a more enraptured stare?
Ah, Miss, in thee I see a lovely prize;
Nor is there one in Eden half so fair.
Kings might long to kiss and e'en caress thee,
Esteemed by all the good—God bless thee.
But I, alas! an uncouth, rustic cuss,
And little schooled to etiquette and such,
I only ask thy friendship firm, and thus
Look upon thee—a friend—I ask not much,
Ever to dream of thee when all alone,
Your form, my queen, I'll kneel before thy throne."

These are but two examples in hundreds that might be given to show how this original man feels, thinks, and writes. Let these illustrations suffice. Now for the outward man as known to the crowds of friends who meet him in every-day life—the true friend, the jolly companion.

Captain Crawford's genealogy is traceable to a Scotch origin. John A. Crawford, the poet scout's father, led rather an eventful life. He was born near Edinburgh, Scotland, in 1816. When fourteen years old he entered a tailoring establishment at Glasgow, and served seven years as an apprentice, and then went to London to finish his trade. After two years he returned to Glasgow. Here he made political speeches, advocated a free form of government, and was banished, a price being put on his head. He fled and hid in Rob Roy's cave, where he was fed for six weeks by an old Scotch lady called Granny McGregor, when a fishing-smack picked him up and carried him to the north coast of Ireland. Here he married Susie Wallace, the daughter of another refugee, and a descendant of Sir William, the Scotch chief. The elder Crawford was a fine tailor, a jolly companion, and a good elocutionist and reciter of Scotch selections. He was a temperate man until he married, when it seems he acquired a taste for strong drink. To escape from dissolute associates, he sailed for America in 1854, leaving his wife and five children, of whom Jack was the third, in Ireland. For four years the mother struggled to support them, receiving little assistance from her husband. Then she left her children with an uncle, James Wallace, and came to America, joining her husband at Miners-ville, Pa. He promised to reform, and partly did so. The children were sent for, and came to Pennsylvania but the father did little for them, and the boys were obliged to work in the coal mines. Here, at the breaking out of the rebellion, we find Jack picking slate at a coal mine at $1.75 per week. His father was one of the first men to respond to the original call for 75,000 volunteers. He served gallantly under Captain George Lawrence, with the Ringgolds. He was twice badly wounded, once at Antietam and once at Cold Harbor. Jack soon ran away, and enlisted when he was not quite sixteen years old. Governor Curtin sent him home twice from Harrisburgh, because he was young and small. He made a third attempt, and joined the 48th Pennsylvania volunteers, getting fully into the war in time to be twice wounded, first at Spottsylvania, May 12th, 1864, and then at Petersburg, April 21, 1865. The severest wound was received at Spottsylvania Court-House while charging the confederate works. He was carried to Washington and later to Saterlee Hospital at West Philadelphia. Here it was that he learned to read and write under the instruction of a Sister of Charity, for the necessity of earning a living for his mother and the other members of the family had deprived him of the advantage of schooling.

His father died very shortly after the war from the effects of a severe wound in the head, received May 18th, 1864. Just before the death of his father he was called upon to bear the stronger bereavement of a mother's death; but before she died she asked him to promise never to drink. This story is best told by Captain Crawford himself. In a letter dated February 26th, 1880, addressed to Colonel Judson, who had in a story made some erroneous statements about him, the Captain says:

"I desire to ask a particular favor of you. . . . In some of your stories you make me say I promised some one six months ago that I would not drink, etc. Now, my dear Colonel, here is where you touch a tender point. I had a sainted, God-fearing, and sweet mother, to whom I owe everything. No one but the Almighty knows what that mother suffered for me and all her children through my father's intemperance. When she was dying she called me to her bedside and asked me to promise her I would never drink intoxicants; and although my lips had never tasted intoxicants before, on my knees, in the presence of my brothers, sisters, and friends, I made her that promise. Colonel, as God is my judge, I have faithfully kept it, and will while I live and breathe."

The Captain has frequently brought such men as Wild Bill to tears by his pathetic recital of this incident in his life. Once Wild Bill said, after hearing Jack recite a poem called "Mother's Prayers," which is based on that promise, "God bless you, Jack; you strike a tender spot, old boy, when you talk mother that way."

Soon after his mother's death Jack became anxious to try his fortunes in the West, stories of which had reached his ears. The death of his mother fell upon him as a heavy blow, but despondency was soon drowned in the ocean of hope that opened up to him. The future seemed rich, and its pleasing possibilities encouraged him to work like a hero. He obtained a letter from General Hartranft, which he subsequently got General Sherman to indorse. Armed with this and similar credentials, the young man started West, where he located, and soon gained the good-will of the frontier military. He soon obtained promotion, and earned the reputation of being a bold, honest, and skilful scout. He was one of the earliest explorers in the Black Hills, chief of the pioneer scouts, and one of the founders of Deadwood, Custer City, Crook, Gayville, and Spearfish. In the Indian campaign of 1876 he was second in the command of General Crook's scouts, and he superseded Buffalo Bill as chief on August 24th of the same year, the latter having resigned. As a scout his record has been signalized by singular acts of bravery. He knows almost every foot of the frontier lands, and he is fearless in the presence of danger. In July, 1876, in response to a telegram, he rode from Medicine Bow, on the U. P. R. R., to Rosebud and Little Big Horn, in the Big Horn Mountains, nearly four hundred miles, through a country peopled with savage Indians. He carried the New York *Herald's* account of the battle of Slim Buttes to Fort Laramie—three hundred and fifty miles—in less than four days. For this he received in all $722.75.

In a letter of introduction given to Captain Crawford, in 1880, by Governor Perkins, of California, the Governor said : "He is known as 'Captain Jack,' a title gained by his devotion and loyalty to the principles of justice, patriotism, and humanity."

Captain Jack holds credentials entitling him to correspond for some of the best daily papers in New York. His letters in many papers have for years attracted attention. Besides letters he has written several sketches for magazines, but he abhors sensational notoriety. He has often appeared in public as a lecturer and reciter of his own poems, always with great success.

The following life-like portrait, by Edward L. Keyes, late lieutenant of the Fifth U. S. Cavalry, will give a fair idea of the man :

"Being in New Mexico last week, and having a day to spare, I decided to renew my acquaintance with Fort Craig, which place I had not seen since I camped there in 1875, *en route* from Arizona to the Indian Territory. Imagine my surprise when the first person to greet me, as I neared the trader's store, was my old friend and quondam companion, Jack Crawford, or 'Captain Jack,' the 'Poet Scout,' as he is now called. The meeting was a pleasure to us both. I had not seen him since we parted in the Black Hills in 1876, at the close of the Sitting Bull expedition, I to return to my post and he to follow a fresher trail farther to the south-west. After learning that he is post trader, postmaster, post-contractor, etc., not to mention his cattle and mining interests, he made me understand that it would be 'bad medicine' for me if I spread my blankets outside of his 'wickiupp,' as he termed his domicile. So I joyfully accepted his insinuating invitation.

"Perhaps I could give you a pen portrait of the celebrated scout. He is a

tall, wiry-built man, with a nervous, sensitive face, which his open, frank de-
meanor dignifies when you have once entered into conversation with him.
His manner is simple and easy, entirely free from affectation. His long, light
brown hair falls below his shoulders, and a mustache and goatee of the same
color ornament his youthful face. A large light felt sombrero crowns his head,
and his body is covered with a blue shirt with wide, flowing collar. Buckskin
trousers with fringed sides cover his long, muscular legs, and a belt, with a
'persuader' attached, usually encircles his waist. He is thirty-eight years of age,
though he does not look it. He was chief of the scouts during the Sitting Bull
expedition, in which I took part. It was during this campaign that he made that
daring and remarkable ride, carrying dispatches alone four hundred miles,
through the midst of the foe, riding at night and hiding in the chaparral during
the day, with the knowledge that if his horse neighed he would be discovered,
captured, and tortured.

"We spent the day in recounting half-forgotten events of the 'horse-meat'
campaign, and again, in fancy, roughing it from the Platte to the Yellowstone,
thence across the Bad Lands to the Black Hills. One incident I recalled which
caused our conversation to take a poetical turn. I remembered that it was Jack
Crawford who, while we lay encamped on War Bonnet Creek, Wyoming,
sent us the sad, shocking intelligence of the gallant Custer's fate. I also
remembered that soon after he reached our camp he entered my tent, and,
throwing himself on my blankets, produced a small blank-book from his pocket,
in which he at once began writing. Though Jack conversed well, his chirog-
raphy was somewhat peculiar. He had never been to school in his life, and at the
time of which I speak writing was a trail which he had only lately struck.
Notwithstanding this, he was busily engaged jotting down his thoughts. And
at last I asked him what he was doing. 'Writing some verses on the death of
Custer,' was his reply. Remembering all this as though it had occurred the
day before, I asked him if his now famous poem on that brave cavalry officer's
tragic death was the result of that morning's inspiration. I learned that it was."

But to go farther is useless. In a limited sketch there can be no complete
picture of such a man. At best there is but an occasional glance, in broken
outline, at the real man. To be properly estimated with his faults, to which
all flesh is heir, and with those qualities which delight thousands who under-
stand him, he must be known. Through all the vicissitudes of fortune, the
changes of time and place, no man can say he ever forgot a friend. He holds to
the saying of Henry Clay, that no new friends can take the place of those we have
long 'tried and loved.' His social qualities charm large circles of admirers, who
are ever anxious to meet him, while his stories of camp and field, and his inex-
haustible fund of original Western anecdotes, enrich his earnest conversation in
a manner singularly pleasing and original.

A CHAPTER FOR BOYS.

I wish I could sit down and take every dime-novel-reading little boy in America by the hand and point out to him the destination he will reach if he persists in reading the vile trash which depicts such Indian scenes as never occurred, and points out "blood-and-thunder" heroes who never lived, and of such a type as were never heard of in the West. If I had the power I would catch every dime-novel publisher in America and confine him in prison for life, where he could not pursue his criminal work—for it is criminal—and lead so many bright boys to ruin and disgrace. My name has never yet figured in one of these trashy concerns with my consent, although I have been offered quite large sums by publishers to allow my name to be used as the author of a Western story which they would have written by another, just as they do with other Western characters whom I could name. It is a great trick on the part of publishers to endeavor to secure the names of noted scouts, hunters, and actors as authors of the most ridiculous trash that was ever printed, and I regret to say that some Western men are so foolish as to bite at their glittering bait. But a few weeks since in a New York publication I was pained and mortified to see an old picture of myself, published with others, with a flash story, and labelled, if I remember rightly, "Broncho Billy."

The first desire of the average boy after reading a story of Western adventure is to go "out West and kill Indians." To a Western man this desire is so absurd and ridiculous as to be really laughable. Poor little innocent dupes! Of the many boys who have abandoned their homes to exterminate Indians not one in a thousand ever reached the

Missouri River, and those who did get beyond that stream invariably went to work in kitchens of hotels washing dishes, or served as lackeys in some subordinate position until their parents could send for them. The poor, blinded boys do not realize that to be efficient in the field as a scout a man must have lived in the West for many years ; must be familiar with every foot of the country, and acquainted with the Indians and their haunts and customs. Neither do they cast a thought upon the hardships and privations of the life of a scout : exposed to piercing cold ; driving, blinding snow storms ; drenching rains ; starvation for days at a time ; intensest heat and tongues parched for water in summer ; always in danger of death and mutilation at the hands of an invisible and cruel foe—these and a thousand other hardships always fall to the lot of a scout on the frontier. The men who follow such a life do not do it so much from a love of adventure as from a love of the big silver dollars which they receive in payment for their services.

Many of the young men in the penitentiaries of the Western States and Territories assert unqualifiedly that they were brought to their present shame and disgrace through reading dime novels. They longed to be heroes or highwaymen or noted robbers, and their first attempt at crime invariably led to their imprisonment for a long term.

Boys, take the earnest advice of a frontiersman, and stay at home. To attempt to gain heroism by following the course pointed out by the publishers of vile novels will lead you to disgrace and death, just as surely as the night follows the declining day. Learn some good trade or profession, and stick to it, and you will grow up beloved and honored by all who know you, and your names may some day be written high up on the glittering scroll of fame. Future Presidents of these great United States are now but boys, and you may be one of them, little reader, if you will apply yourself to study, acquire the principles of truth and manhood, and endeavor to fit yourself for the position. Try it, little friend, and avoid those damnable dime novels as you would a venomous, hideous rattlesnake. They are more dangerous.

"MUSTERED OUT."

The following impromptu lines are from the pen of Captain "Jack" Crawford, the "Poet Scout."—*N. Y. Evening Telegram, August 7th*, 1885:

A NATION droops her head and weeps ;
  Her tears are honest drops of sorrow ;
Her honored chief in silence sleeps ;
  We march behind his bier to-morrow.

To-morrow you who often stood
  Beside him in the fiercest fray
Will humbly bow, for God is good,
  Since all can honor him to-day.

His valor as a soldier boy,
  His dauntless courage as our chief,
His honesty without alloy,
  Will ever stand in bold relief.

Yes, comrades, he is mustered out ;
  His feet have pressed the golden stair,
His soul has passed o'er heaven's redoubt,
  To be promoted over there.

THE HEROES DEPARTED.

Dedicated to my Comrades of the G. A. R.

COME back, oh come back to us, heroes departed,
   Come back to us comrades and pass in review,
Come back, silent chieftain, your comrades are waiting
   To join with the angels in honor of you.

We muster to-day but a few of that army
   You led on to victory on many a field,
And we feel that thy spirit will hover around us,
   Our star that will guide and our hope that will shield.

We honor thee, first, as our greatest commander,
   Transferred in advance to that heavenly corps :
Tell Reno and Sedgwick, tell Burnside and Hooker,
   Tell Abe we are coming a million and more.

Tell Washington. Warren, tell Baker and Kearney,
   Tell Meade, and my own beloved colonel who fell
While leading our old Forty-eighth through red blazes,
   Right over the ramparts and into Fort Hell.

Yes, tell them we're coming, we make no distinction—
   The private who fell with the colors in hand,
The boy with his drum who has answered death's tattoo,
   Are equal to kings in that greater command.

And if you can look from the ramparts of heaven,
   To-day your old comrades will pass in review,
Not *en masse*, not in column, but scattered and straggling,
   Deployed at the front, but all coming to you.

And you who are draping our dear starry banner,
   That flag of our Union, you fought to maintain,
Oh, let treason assail it, though aged and hoary,
   And you would go marching to glory again !

But hark ! 'tis the voice of the mocking-bird singing
   A sweet song of peace from the cold cannon's mouth,

And the soldier who fought with his back to the southward
  Shakes hands with the one who stood face to the South.

The brave meet the brave while true feelings fraternal
  Leap into the hearts of the gray and the blue,
And Johnny cries, "Billy, while you-uns whipped we-uns,
  Oh, we-uns war makin' it sultry for you.

"Let bitterness reign among them as war missin',
  When minies war singin' a dirge o'er the brave ;
For you-uns are happy and we-uns ain't sorry,
  "Tis the land of the free, not the home of the slave."

With malice toward none and with *Charity* blended,
  Fraternity, Loyalty, peace and good-will,
We gather to-day to assist one another,
  If need be, in climbing adversity's hill.

And oh, my dear comrades, look well to the loved ones,
  The soldiers' bequest who have answered tattoo ;
Be kind to the widow, be kind to the orphan,
  And the Great Chief of all will deal kindly with you.

A touch of the elbow with shoulder to shoulder,
  A flash of the eye and the grasp of the hand,
And the soul of the soldier is filled with emotions,
  That none but the brave and the true understand.

Oh, comrades, forgive me, nor think it is weakness
  That causes these teardrops to spring to my eyes,
'Tis the purest, the holiest thoughts of a soldier
  Who never yet flinched, and who needs no disguise.

But think of the chair of our chieftain now vacant,
  So silent at roll call, so sad and so drear ;
While the angel of death will still add to his roster,
  And many now filled will be vacant next year.

And when after taps comes the last reveille,
  And "assembly" shall sound from that far-away shore,
May we meet on parade 'neath the shade of life's tree,
  With Grant, silent chief, at the head of the corps.

THE MINER'S HOME.

It is not a castle with towering walls,
With marble floor and stately halls,
With lovely walks and grand old trees,
Nodding and bending in the breeze.

No : his home is an humble cot,
Perched perchance on the mountain top,
With tunnels beneath, where the iron horse
Thunders along on his fiery course.

Fair Virginia ! above the hill,
Where miners dig with pick and drill,
Where honest toilers seek to rest
Their weary bones upon thy breast.

A loving wife to make one glad,
A babe to kiss the miner lad ;
With this the miner need not roam,
If he has a cottage and love at home.

Mine, though far away from here,
My cabin home is ever dear.
Bright memories haunt me every day
Of that cabin where I often lay,

And dreamed of eyes of heavenly blue —
A maiden young and fair and true ;
Of brighter days and toil's reward,
A maiden's love for a mountain bard.

Up the mountain, down the glen,
Each eve I see these hardy men ;
With axe and shovel, pick and drill,
They toil all day with a hearty will.

And when at e'en their toil is o'er,
They hasten home to the open door

Of the little cot ; though shaggy and grim,
There's happiness there and love within.

Though the rooms within are low and small,
There's whitewash on the old gray wall ;
The table with its crockery, too,
Is glistening like the morning dew.

While all seem happy in the cot,
The children, sporting on the lot,
Are merry as a marriage bell,
And mother whispers, " All is well."

And now good-bye—I must away,
My time is up.   Yet while I say
Good-bye, I'll wish, where'er I roam,
That GOD will bless *the miner's home.*

RATTLIN' JOE'S PRAYER.

JIST pile on some more o' them pine knots,
   An' squat yoursel's down on this skin,
An', Scotty, let up on yer growlin'—
   The boys are all tired o' yer chin.
Alleghany, jist pass round the bottle,
   An' give the lads all a square drink,
An' as soon as yer settled I'll tell ye
   A yarn as 'll please ye, I think.

'Twas the year eighteen hundred an' sixty,
   A day in the bright month o' June,
When the Angel o' Death from the Diggin's
   Snatched " Monte Bill "—known as McCune.
Wal, Bill war a favorite among us,
   In spite o' the trade that he had,
Which war gamblin' ; but—don't you forget it—
   He of'en made weary hearts glad ;

An', pards, while he lay in that coffin,
  Which we hewed from the trunk o' a tree,
His face war as calm as an angel's,
  An' white as an angel's could be.

An' thar's war the trouble commenced, pards.
  Thar war no gospel-sharps in the camps,
An' Joe said : " We can't drop him this way,
  Without some directions or stamps."
Then up spoke old Sandy McGregor :
  " Look 'ee yar, mates, I'm reg'lar dead stuck,
I can't hold no hand at religion,
  An' I'm 'feared Bill's gone in out o' luck.
If I knowed a darn thing about prayin',
  I'd chip in an' say him a mass ;
But I ain't got no show in the lay-out,
  I can't beat the game, so I pass."

Rattlin' Joe war the next o' the speakers,
  An' Joe war a friend o' the dead ;
The salt water stood in his peepers,
  An' these are the words as he said :
" Mates, ye know as I ain't any Christian,
  An' I'll gamble the good Lord don't know
That thar lives sich a rooster as I am ;
  But thar once war a time, long ago,
When I war a kid ; I remember,
  My old mother sent me to school,
To the little brown church every Sunday,
  Whar they said I was dumb as a mule.
An' I reckon I've nearly forgotten
  Purty much all thet ever I knew.
But still, if ye'll drop to my racket,
  I'll show ye jist what I kin do.

" Now, I'll show you *my* bible," said Joseph—
  " Jist hand me them cards off that rack ;
I'll convince ye thet this *are* a bible,"
  An' he went to work shufflin' the pack.

He spread out the cards on the table,
　An' begun kinder pious-like : " Pards,
If ye'll jist choose yer racket an' listen,
　I'll show ye the pra'ar-book in cards.

"The ' ace,' that reminds us of one God,
　The ' deuce,' of the Father an' Son,
The ' tray,' of the Father an' Son, Holy Ghost,
　For, ye see, all them three are but one.
The ' four-spot ' is Matthew, Mark, Luke an' John,
　The ' five-spot,' the virgins who trimmed
Their lamps while yet it was light of the day,
　And the five foolish virgins who sinned.
The ' six-spot '—in six days the Lord made the world,
　The sea and the stars in the heaven ;
He saw it war good w'at He made, then He said,
　I'll jist go the rest on the ' seven.'
The ' eight-spot ' is Noah, his wife an' three sons,
　An' Noah's three sons had their wives ;
God loved the hull mob, so bid 'em emb-ark—
　In the freshet He saved all their lives.
The nine war the lepers of biblical fame,
　A repulsive an' hideous squad—
The ' ten ' are the holy commandments, which came
　To us perishin' creatures from God.
The ' queen ' war of Sheba in old Bible times,
　The ' king' represents old King Sol.
She brought in a hundred young folks, gals an' boys,
　To the King in his government ball.
They were all dressed alike, an' she axed the old boy
　(She'd put up his wisdom as bosh)
Which war boys an' which gals.　Old Sol. said : ' By Joe,
　How dirty their hands !　Make 'em wash ! '
An' then he showed Sheba the boys only washed
　Their hands and a part o' their wrists,
While the gals jist went up to their elbows in suds.
　Sheba weakened an' shook the king's fists.
Now, the ' knave,' that's the Devil, an', God, ef ye please,
　Jist keep his hands off'n poor Bill.

An' now, lads, jist drop on yer knees for a while
   Till I draw, and perhaps I kin fill ;
An' hevin' no Bible, I'll pray on the cards,
   Fur I've showed ye they're all on the squar',
An' I think God 'll cotton to all that I say,
   If I'm only sincere in the pra'ar.
Jist give him a corner, good Lord—not on stocks,
   Fur I ain't such a durned fool as that,
To ax ye fur anything worldly fur Bill,
   Kase ye'd put me up then fur a flat.
I'm lost on the rules o' yer game, but I'll ax
   Fur a seat fur him back o' the throne,
And I'll bet my hull stack thet the boy'll behave
   If yer angels jist lets him alone.
Thar's nuthin' bad 'bout him unless he gets riled—
   The boys 'll all back me in that—
But if any one treads on his corns, then you bet
   He'll fight at the drop o' the hat.
Jist don't let yer angels run over him, Lord,
   Nor shut off all to once on his drink ;
Break him in kinder gentle an' mild on the start,
   An he'll give ye no trouble, I think.
An' couldn't ye give him a pack of old cards,
   To amuse himself once in a while?
But I warn ye right hyar, not to bet on his game,
   Or he ll get right away with yer pile.
An' now, Lord, I hope thet ye've tuck it all in,
   An' listened to all thet I've said.
I know that my prayin' is jist a bit thin,
   But I've done all I kin for the dead.
An' I hope I hain't troubled yer Lordship too much—
   So I'll cheese it by axin' again
Thet ye won't let the ' knave ' git his grip on poor Bill.
   Thet's all, Lord—yours truly—Amen."

Thet's " Rattlin' Joe's'' prayer, old pardners,
   An'—what ! you all snorin' ? Say, Lew,
By thunder ! I've talked every rascal to sleep,
   So I guess I hed best turn in too.

THE TENDERFOOT.

A SONG.

Look not with contempt on his dust-covered form,
  Or his coat, tho' 'tis shabby and gray,
But think of the heart that is swelling beneath,
  And the loved ones he left far away.
He comes not with wealth, but his muscles are strong,
  And his face bears the stamp of a man ;
Perhaps he has little ones praying at home—
  Then help him whenever you can.

Chorus.

Yes, help the poor tenderfoot, give him a show—
  Some day he may be a great man ;
Perhaps he has little ones praying at home—
  Then help him whenever you can.

Sometimes a kind word to the poor and oppressed
  Will lighten the burden of care,
And shed a new light on a heart that is sad,
  And make all his prospects more fair.
It costs a man nothing to speak a kind word
  To the tenderfoot—strange in our land—
For oh ! if you knew how it brightens his life,
  You would not refuse him a hand.
                                        Chorus.

He is poor in his pocket but rich—in his mind,
  He is filled with ambition and hope.
Who knows—he may strike it, as others have done,
  And make a big raise on the slope.
There's Mackey and Fair, there's Flood and O'Brien,
  There's Tabor, and Routt, and McKay ;
Just think of the power they wield in our land
  They were all tenderfeet in their day.
                                        Chorus.

LITTLE ONES PRAYING AT HOME.

A SONG.

On the 15th of September, 1880, I was camped at Lake Goozman, " *Laguna de Goozman*," in the State of Chihuahua, Old Mexico. I had been sent out by General Buell, with two companions, to find the camp of the hostile chief Victorio, with the view of meeting him, and, if possible, of inducing him to return to the Reservation. While reading a letter from my wife, the following line appeared: "Remember, my dear boy, *you have little ones praying at home*." As this was one of the most dangerous as well as the most t'resome trips I ever made, these lines were very suggestive, and there, by the beautiful lake and by the light of the moon, I wrote the following song:

> THERE are little ones praying for me far away,
>   There are little ones praying for me ;
> With tiny hands pressed before each little breast,
>   Their sweet faces in dreamland I see.
> Bless papa, dear father, where'er he may go,
>   And where duty may call him to roam ;
> Through the hills or the valleys of Old Mexico,
>   Watch over and bring him safe home.

> *Chorus.*

> So to-night I am happy in Old Mexico,
>   While I sit in the moonlight alone ;
> For surely 'tis pleasant to feel and to know
>   There are little ones praying at home.

> I know not what moment my spirit may fly
>   To that land where dear mother has gone ;
> But oh, if I knew on that bosom so true
>   I might rest on the morrow at dawn,
> I would willingly go, never more to return,
>   Never more through these wild lands to roam ;
> But sweet little voices seem whispering to-night,
>   " You have little ones praying at home."

> *Chorus.*

The moon in her splendor is shining to-night,
  By her beams I am writing just now,
While an angel of love seems to smile from above,
  With the bright star of hope on her brow,
And whisper in language so sweet to my soul,
  " I am with you wherever you roam ;
And remember when weary and foot-sore at night,
  You have little ones praying at home.''

                                        Chorus.

———

BALD MOUNTAIN.

(CARIBOO, B. C.)

WHAT mighty mountains I behold
  Where'er I turn my eyes,
Undoubted evidence of gold,
  With snow peaks in the skies ;
And down below green pasture land,
  Where cooling streamlets flow,
I never gazed on sight so grand
  As this I see below.

What mean those giant ledges there
  With mossy-covered brow ?
And, tell me, are there none that bear
  The gold we're seeking now ?
The little streamlets seem to frown ;
  I almost hear them say,
" For ages we have washed it down
  Where miners struck the pay.''

And Nature ought to teach us, too,
  If we could read aright,
That every ounce from Cariboo
  Came down some rugged height ;

And though our sky is looking dark,
　　Our quartz is yet untried,
Remember that Noah built an ark
　　To float upon the tide !

And surely you, old pioneers
　　(Who came in times of old),
Will only laugh at idle fears,
　　And never lose your hold ;
For one who never turned a drill
　　And never fired a shot,
Can little know what's in the hill
　　Except for some vile plot.

But so it is in every land :
　　Wherever gold is found,
There're thieving tricksters right on hand
　　To run it in the ground ;
And you who toil from morn till night—
　　Will you give up the ship
When you have got a stake in sight—
　　Let go and lose your grip ?

Thou crystal bed, half decomposed,
　　With walls six feet apart,
We ask no wise philosopher
　　To tell us what thou art.
'Tis but the miner can unfold
　　Thy secret, as we know,
And wrest from thee the precious gold
　　Thy bosom holds below.

Go ask the winds, ye grumbling drones,
　　If all you've heard is true—
If all your quartz is barren stones
　　In all your Cariboo ?
And they will bleakly answer back,
　　" Go, learn in Nature's school ;
Go, take your pick and bend your back,
　　But don't consult a fool."

THE MOUNTAIN BOY'S LETTER.

Soon after General Grant landed at San Francisco, on his tour around the world, Lincoln Post, G. A. R., presented the "Color Guard," a military drama, in which Captain Jack Crawford played the leading *rôle* (a Tennessee scout), supported by T. W. Keene and the California Theatre Company. During the performance Captain Jack recited the "Mountain Boy's Letter" amid great enthusiasm. It was highly appreciated by the General, who, being "corralled," as Jack expresses it, by big bugs and Sunday soldiers, could not reach the boys

> " Who followed him into the battle,
> And gallantly guarded the flanks."

The poem was telegraphed across the continent, and appeared in Grant's "Tour of the World," published in Chicago, and, with the exception of Bret Harte's "Heathen Chinee," is the only poem ever wired from ocean to ocean.— *Will L. Vischer, in Denver Tribune.*

DEAR GINER'L :
I arn't no scollar,

An' I never done nothin' to brag,
    'Cept this—I war one o' the outfit
      As fought for our Star-Spangled Flag.
An' to-day while yer toasted by scollars,
      An' big bugs as make a great noise,
Why, I thought it the squar' thing to write yer,
      An' chip in a word for yer boys.

Cos, yer see, we ain't got the colat'r'l,
      Nor the larnin' to dish it up right ;
But ye'll find should thar be any trouble,
      Our boys are still ready ter fight.
As for you, if they didn't corral yer,
      You'd shake comrades' hands that yer seed,
An' that's why I wanted to tell yer,
      We'll jest take the will for the deed.

But yer back, and the men of *all nations*
      War proud ter do honor to you,
An' I reckon, Ulysses, yer told em,
      Ye wor proud o' yer comrades in blue,

For *you*, we are sure, of all others,
   Remembered our boys in the ranks,
Who follor'd ye inter the battle,
   And gallantly guarded the flanks.

So, welcome, a thousand times welcome,
   Our land is ablaze with delight ;
Our people give thanks for yer safety,
   Your comrades are happy to-night.
We know you are wearied and tuckerd,
   But seein' as you're a new-comer,
You'll *Grant* us one glance on *this line if*,
   In reading, *it takes yer all summer.*

NOTES IN A CAMP-MEETING.

(NEAR WILLIAMSPORT, PA.)

I HAVE heard the different preachers,
   In the camp among the trees,
And the voices of the angels,
   Seeming wafted with the breeze ;
And I'm sure the God of Battles
   Smiled on those who came for good—
But I fear He frowned on many
   Who were wicked, vain, and rude.

The demon Rum I saw, too,
   As he staggered through the camp,
And the crowds who drank in darkness,
   For they shunned the lighted lamp.
There were many Williamsporters—
   And how they cursed and swore !
And I noticed quite a number
   From your moral Jersey shore.

Now, the camp is good for Christians,
  And for those who wish to come
To the crystal fount of Jesus ;
  And I know that there are some
Who have sought and found a Saviour,
  Who was heretofore unknown ;
But I prefer the wilderness,
  To pray to Him alone.

And often in the wildwood,
  And on the far-off plain,
Where, all alone, so oft I've been,
  And soon will be again—
'Twas there, when shades of evening
  And twilight round me fell—
Yes, there alone with angels,
  I thought of heaven and hell !

And when in camp, last evening,
  And sitting 'neath the trees,
I was taking notes of incidents,
  And thought how hard to please,
If Christ Himself came down to preach
  And cure the sin-diseased,
There's some who would not hear Him,
  And some would be displeased !

But there is one thing certain,
  And I'll tell you on the square—
I've seen some preachers put on style
  With such a foreign air ;
And some with stand-up collars
  Would a ragged sinner scorn !
They came out from the city
  To blow their gospel horn !

They told us, too, what they had done
  In other fields of grace—
How many sinners *they* had saved
  From the tormenting-place ;

But there is none that *I* have met
  Who'd risk his scalp with me,
And go convert the noble Sioux
  For smaller salary !

Give me the brave old pioneers—
  The heroes good and bold—
Who never feared to fight and die
  For Christ and His little fold !
The men who left their homes, their all,
  The savage wilds to fight—
Who felled the forest trees by day
  And preached us Christ by night.

Such is the man I love to meet,
  Whose face wears Heaven's brand—
With manly courage in his heart
  And rifle in his hand.
And if some of these dainty preachers
  Cared less for wounds and scars,
Would go out West and preach Christ there,
  We'd have less Indian wars !

But if I've judged them wrongly,
  Oh, pardoned may I be ;
But they're not just the kind of preachers
  To convert such men as we.
Of course, we've no book learning,
  But then our hearts are right—
If we don't know much of preaching,
  We at least know how to fight !

So, Bill, old man, and you, Jack,
  Away to the front and flank ;
You must again face that danger
  From which you never shrank ;
And if they won't send preachers
  To convert the savage state,
Of course the knife and bullet
  Must be the red man's fate.

DREAMING OF MOTHER.

SONG.

LAST night I was dreaming of mother,
  Yes, dreaming of mother and home,
The little log hut where she blessed me
  When fortune compelled me to roam ;
How she prayed for her boy at that moment,
  While tears wet the locks on my brow,
And I said the good-by to my sister,
  Farewell to the farm and the plough !

Chorus.

    Dreaming, dreaming,
      Dreaming of home and of mother ;
    Dreaming of home wherever I roam,
      I'm dreaming of home and of mother.

Last night I was dreaming of mother,
  I dreamed she was free from all care,
And she kissed me again as in childhood
  At home, in the old arm-chair ;
And the old-fashioned cap, like a snowflake
  That mixed with the ringlets of gray,
Seemed richer to me than those treasures
  And millions just over the way.

                      Chorus.

And oft while asleep in the wildwood
  Those scenes of my childhood appear,
And surely the angels are watching
  While dreaming that mother is near !
Oh, happy the thought, dearest mother,
  The hope of our meeting once more,
When, free from the world and its sorrows,
  We dwell on that ever bright shore !

                      Chorus.

CALIFORNIA JOE AND THE GIRL TRAPPER.

A CAMP-FIRE REMINISCENCE.

About the middle of April, 1876, I received a note from California Joe, who had a fine ranche on Rapid Creek, and was trying to induce new-comers to settle there and build a town, to be called Rapid City. The note was written in lead-pencil, and ran thus:

"RAPID, April 10, 1876.

"MY DEAR JACK: If you can be spared for a week from Custer, come over and bring Jule and Frank Smith with you. The reds have been raising merry old h—l, and, after wounding our herder and a miner named Sherwood, got away with eight head of stock, my old Bally with the rest. There are only ten of us here, all told, and I think if you can come with the two boys, we can lay for them at the lower falls, and gobble 'em next time. Answer by bearer if you can't come; and send me fifty rounds of cartridges for the Sharps—big fifty. Hoping this will find you with your top-knot still waving, I remain as ever, your pard, JOE."

I immediately saw Major Wynkoop, commanding the Rangers, got his permission, and arrived at Rapid Creek on the following night, with four comrades. After two days' and nights' watching at the lower falls, Jule Seminole, one of my scouts, a Cheyenne, came in at dusk and informed us that there were between twenty and thirty Indians encamped at the box elder, about twenty miles away, and that they were coming from the direction of the Big Cheyenne, and would probably move to Rapid during the night. Jule could almost invariably tell just what an Indian was going to do if he could get his eyes on him, and he was correct in this instance. About three o'clock next morning Joe went up to his cabin and started a big log fire; also two other fires in different cabins. These cabins were over a mile from where we were in ambush, while our horses were all picketed a quarter of a mile down the creek, which was narrow at its point of entrance from the prairie, but widened into a beautiful river half a mile up. Just as day was breaking, one of the Indians was discovered by Frank Smith wading up the creek. Frank reported to Joe and I, and Joe remarked: "Let him go—he will soon signal the others to follow." In fifteen minutes more the shrill bark of a coyote proved Joe's judgment to be correct. Twenty-three well-armed Indians—Sioux—rode up along the willow bank in Indian file. There were seventeen of us, Zeb Swaringen and Ned Baker, two old miners, having joined us the night before. We had six men on one side, near an opening, which we believed the Indians would break for on receiving our fire from the opposite side; and farther up, when the Indians had got parallel with our main body, we took aim as best we could in the gray of the morning.

and fired nearly together; then, before they recovered, gave them another volley, and, leaving our cover, followed on foot those who did not stay with us. We were disappointed in their taking the opening, but the boys were in fair range and did good work, killing one, wounding two, and unhorsing three others, who took to the woods. We got fifteen ponies, our first fire never touching horse hair, but emptying several saddles. Out of the twenty-three Indians, fifteen escaped. Joe killed three himself with his big Sharps rifle, the last one being nearly five hundred yards away when he fired from a rest off Frank Smith's shoulder. Joe had a piece taken out of his left thigh, Franklin was wounded in the left arm, and the writer slightly scratched near the guard of the right arm. Nobody was seriously hurt, and we had eight scalps to crown our victory. But I did not intend, when I commenced, to write all these particulars; I merely intended to speak of a camp-fire story, as told by Joe at the camp-fire on he night following the incident related. The following lines, as nearly as I can recollect, tell the story of Joe's courtship and marriage. I must add that Joe was killed at Red Cloud, in December the same year, while acting as Black Hills guide. He was a brave, generous, unselfish man, and his only fault was liquor. Now for the story :

> WELL, mates, I don't like stories,
>   Nor am I going to act
> A part around this camp-fire
>   That ain't a truthful fact.
> So fill your pipes and listen,
>   I'll tell you—let me see,
> I think it was in Fifty,
>   From that till Sixty-three.
>
> You've all heard tell of Bridger,
>   I used to run with Jim,
> And many a hard day's scouting
>   I've done 'longside of him.
> Well, once, near old Fort Reno,
>   A trapper used to dwell ;
> We called him old Pap Reynolds—
>   The scouts all knew him well.
>
> One night—the spring of Fifty—
>   We camped on Powder River,
> We killed a calf of buffalo,
>   And cooked a slice of liver :

While eating, quite contented,
  We heard three shots or four ;
Put out the fire and listened,
  Then heard a dozen more.

We knew that old man Reynolds
  Had moved his traps up here ;
So, picking up our rifles
  And fixing on our gear,

We mounted quick as lightnin',
  To save was our desire.
Too late ; the painted heathens
  Had set the house on fire.

We tied our horses quickly,
  And waded up the stream ;
While close beside the water
  I heard a muffled scream.
And there among the bushes
  A little girl did lie.
I picked her up and whispered :
  " I'll save *you, or I'll die !*"

Lord, what a ride ! old Bridger,
  He covered my retreat.
Sometimes the child would whisper,
  In voice so low and sweet :
" Poor papa, God will take him
  To mamma up above ;
There's no one left to love me—
  There's no one left to love."

The little one was thirteen,
  And I was twenty-two.
Said I : " I'll be your father,
  And love you just as true."
She nestled to my bosom,
  Her hazel eyes, so bright,
Looked up and made me happy,
  Though close pursued that night.

A month had passed, and Maggie
  (We called her Hazel Eye),
In truth, was going to leave me—
  Was going to say " good-by."
Her uncle, mad Jack Reynolds—
  Reported long since dead—
Had come to claim my angel,
  His brother's child, he said.

What could I say ? We parted.
  Mad Jack was growing old ;
I handed him a bank-note
  And all I had in gold
They rode away at sunrise,
  I went a mile or two,
And, parting, said : " We'll meet again—
  May God watch over you."

*   *   *   *   *

Beside a laughing, dancing brook,
  A little cabin stood,
As, weary with a long day's scout,
  I spied it in the wood.
A pretty valley stretched beyond,
  The mountains towered above,
While near the willow bank I heard
  The cooing of a dove.

'Twas one grand panorama,
  The brook was plainly seen,
Like a long thread of silver
  In a cloth of lovely green.
The laughter of the waters,
  The cooing of the dove,
Was like some painted picture—
  Some well-told tale of love.

While drinking in the grandeur,
  And resting in my saddle,
I heard a gentle ripple
  Like the dipping of a paddle.
I turned toward the eddy—
  A strange sight met my view :
A maiden, with her rifle,
  In a little bark canoe.

She stood up in the centre,
　The rifle to her eye ;
I thought (just for a second)
　My time had come to die.
I doffed my hat and told her
　(If it was all the same)
To drop her little shooter,
　For I was not her game.

She dropped the deadly weapon,
  And leaped from the canoe.
Said she : " I beg your pardon,
  I thought you were a Sioux ;
Your long hair and your buckskin
  Looked warrior-like and rough ;
My bead was spoiled by sunshine,
  Or I'd killed you, sure enough."

"Perhaps it had been better
  You dropped me then," said I ;
" For surely such an angel
  Would bear me to the sky."
She blushed and dropped her eyelids,
  Her cheeks were crimson red ;
One half-shy glance she gave me,
  And then hung down her head.

I took her little hand in mine—
  She wondered what I meant,
And yet she drew it not away,
  But rather seemed content.
We sat upon the mossy bank—
  Her eyes began to fill—
The brook was rippling at our feet,
  The dove was cooing still.

I smoothed her golden tresses,
  Her eyes looked up in mine,
She seemed in doubt—then whispered :
  " 'Tis such a long, long time
Strong arms were thrown around me—
  I'll save you, or I'll die."
I clasped her to my bosom—
  My long-lost Hazel Eye.

The rapture of that moment
  Was almost heaven to me.
I kissed her 'mid her tear-drops,
  Her innocence and glee.

Her heart near mine was beating,
　　While sobbingly she said :
" My dear, my brave preserver,
　　They told me you were dead.

" But, oh ! those parting words, Joe,
　　Have never left my mind.
You said : ' We'll meet again, Mag,'
　　Then rode off like the wind.
And, oh ! how I have prayed, Joe,
　　For you, who saved my life,
That God would send an angel
　　To guard you through all strife.

" And he who claimed me from you,
　　My uncle, good and true—
Now sick in yonder cabin—
　　Has talked so much of you.
' If Joe were living, darling,'
　　He said to me last night,
' He would care for Maggie
　　When God puts out my light.' "

We found the old man sleeping.
　　" Hush ! Maggie, let him rest."
The sun was slowly sinking
　　In the far-off glowing west ;
And, though we talked in whispers,
　　He opened wide his eyes.
" A dream—a dream !" he murmured,
　　" Alas ! a dream of lies !"

She drifted like a shadow
　　To where the old man lay.
" You had a dream, dear uncle—
　　Another dream to-day ?"
" Oh, yes ; I saw an angel,
　　As pure as mountain snow,
And near her, at my bed-side,
　　Stood California Joe."

" I'm sure *I'm* not an angel,
   Dear uncle, that you know ;
These arms are brown, my hands, too—
   My face is not like snow.
Now, listen, while I tell you,
   For I have news to cheer,
And Hazel Eye is happy,
   For Joe is truly here."

And when, a few days after,
   The old man said to me :
" Joe, boy, *she ar'* a angel,
   An' good as angels be.
For three long months she's hunted
   An' trapped an' nurs'd me, too ;
God bless ye, boy ! I believe it—
   She's safe along wi' you."

    *   *   *   *   *

The sun was slowly sinking
   When Mag (my wife) and I
Came riding through the valley,
   The tear-drops in her eye.
" One year ago to-day, Joe—
   I see the mossy grave—
We laid him 'neath the daisies,
   My uncle, good and brave."

And, comrades, every spring-time
   Was sure to find me there—
A something in that valley
   Was always fresh and fair.
Our loves were newly kindled
   While sitting by the stream,
Where two hearts were united
   In love's sweet, happy dream.

YOU ARE WANTED AT HOME.

SONG AND CHORUS.

Written in San Francisco while awaiting the arrival of General Grant from his tour around the world, and afterward sung to the General by the California Quartette.

You are wanted at home, gallant chieftain,
We are watching and waiting for thee,
We are waiting to give you a greeting,
A welcome from over the sea—
A welcome as soldiers can give it,
Who marched with you back to the dome,
We will show you, our noble commander,
How much you are wanted at home.

Chorus.

You are wanted at home, yes, we want you,
For you were our bright guiding star,
You would guide us aright in our duty
In peace, as you led us in war.

You are wanted at home—do you wonder
That comrades all shout with delight?
It is love for our gallant commander
Who led us in many a fight.
It is you who can best understand us,
Our chieftain, from over the foam.
And now you are here, we will tell you
The why you are wanted at home.

Chorus.

You are wanted at home—'tis the *Union*,
The land and the home of the brave,
The land of our star-spangled banner,
Where man nevermore can be slave.
You are wanted by hearts true and loyal,
Who love you, wherever you roam,
And you will be happy returning,
Because there is no place like home.

Chorus.

TRUTH.

Truth is like gold in the gulches,
  Oft buried deep under the sod,
While often the tender-foot * searches
  For gold on the face of the clod.
The color is found on the surface,
  But if you would find richer stock,
Go down where large nuggets are buried,
  Go down till you find the bed-rock.

Many people examine the surface,
  And penetrate never within ;
But the outside is sleek as a beaver,
  The heart often dyed deep in sin.
Hence lives are but base contradictions,
  And hearts are oft pining in sorrow ;
To-day what may seem quite angelic
  As crime may be looked on to-morrow.

Truth, then, is scattered and buried,
  It is mixed with the gold in the glen ;
Go wash all the dirt from these nuggets,
  And find if you can honest men.
For truth that is pure and unvarnished
  Is worthy the search of the wise ;
Compare it with nuggets and diamonds,
  Pure truth is by far the best prize.

One miner, perhaps, in a million
  Will pick up a fortune to-day,
While others may toil for a lifetime,
  Yet delve in the very same way.
And yet 'tis by toiling we find them—
  These nuggets we so much desire ;
'Tis only by working unceasing
  We manage to climb up still higher.

* A new-comer.

And yet truth may sparkle like diamonds,
  But some men will cast it aside,
And, instead, they will treasure the mica,
  And say to the truth, " Let her slide."
But truth is the old rock of ages
  Upon which our forefathers stood.
Without it there must be corruption,
  And with it our lives must be good.

THE HAPPY-GO-LUCKY TRAMP.

WHAT am I doin'? Now, what is't yer biz?
  Can't a feller stand here on the corner an' think?
Thunder ! I ain't no slouch, an' as to my phiz,
  It's a little off-color. What's that? Too much drink?
Wal, I reckon yer right ; but, look ye, my friend,
  Yer a stranger to me, an' yer one of the few
As would stop for a second. They don't condescend
  To grant such as me but a short interview.

Don't talk like that, sir, it ain't jest the thing
  To speak of one's mother, and she so long dead.
This of'n reminds me—this little gold ring—
  Jest now I was thinkin' it must go for bread.
An' I've worn it so long—great God ! when I think
  How it served to remind me—"while tossed on life's tide"—
Of that angel who gave it—why, even in drink
  She comes to me, speaks to me, prays by my side.

No, no, wait a minute, I can't drink just yet,
  Le's talk of that last ride I took on the freight—
Forget ! Man alive, I don't want to forget,
  But there—never mind—I won't ask you to wait,

For I reckon it ain't interestin' nor new,
    Thar are so many tramps, but my own brother Ned—
Why, stranger, thar's somethin' the matter with you!
    Oh, I thought as it mout a-bin somethin' I said.

What started me drinkin'? Wal, that's quite a yarn,
    An', besides, I don't want ter have you standin' here—
Howsomever, I reckon you don't care a darn—
    But them fancy-dressed ladies, jest see how they stare!
What's that you say? Oh, don't make no error,
    Jest show me a cup of hot coffee and strong—
God bless you! my heart's fairly jumpin' with terror
    For fear you'll back out as we're joggin' along.

Good flavor? You bet it is the way-uppest coffee
    · I've struck in a month. But I can't understand
Why you—oh, all right—so you think that I'm off, eh?
    What! me, a tramp, live on the fat of the land!
Ha! ha! Blast your eyes, man, I'd sooner to-morrow
    Be found in that tail-race, all crushed by the wheel,
Than add one more sin to my cup full of sorrow—
    And so, you would tempt a poor devil to steal?

Not a sup?—not a bite! Oh, why will temptation
    Keep trailin' me up! Get out of my sight!
Or I swar by my soul there will be a sensation,
    And I will get grub in the cooler to-night!
What's that? You know me of old? You're another!
    And, hang you! if I wasn't weaker'n water,
I'd— What!— Git out!— You!— You, Ned!— My brother!
    I reckon I'm crazy, and that's what's the matter!

Corral me if I didn't think you wor dead, boy.
    Why, darn yer young hide, Ned, but whar hev ye bin?
I thought ye were plugged with an ounce of cold lead, boy;
    Ye must hev slipped out 'fore the redskins got in.
What's that? In the "Happy-go-Lucky" you struck it!
    The mischief you did! Well, somehow I knew,
The last time I helped ye to pull up that bucket
    Thar war ducats right thar for your brother and you!

OUR PROSPECT.

There's a bonny wee spot in the mountains I love,
Where the pine trees are waving o'erhead far above,
Where the miners are happy, kind-hearted and free,
And many come here from way over the sea.

There's gold in the mountains, there's gold in each glen,
The good time is coming, have patience, brave men ;
Hold on to your ledges, and soon you will see
Both money and mills coming over the sea.

I have seen your Bonanza, your great Cariboo ;
I've been in your tunnels, but everything's new ;
I've stood at the face of your wondrous Lowhee,
And find that the prospects are good as can be.

Don't think that Victoria will give you a hand,
Nor furnish a baw-bee to prospect your land.
The miner must prospect and show the gold free,
Then capital comes from way over the sea.

Now take my advice, and I'm in with you, too,
Just stick to your ledges, whatever you do ;
Don't worry and fret, if at first you don't see
A fortune in sight, for it's coming to thee.

BARKERVILLE, B. C.

WILD BILL'S GRAVE.

On the side of the hill, between Whitewood and Deadwood,
    At the foot of the pine stump, there lies a lone grave,
Environed with rocks and with pine trees and redwood,
    Where the wild roses bloom o'er the breast of the brave.
A mantle of brushwood the green sward incloses,
    The green boughs are waving far up overhead ;
While under the sod and the flow'rets reposes
            The brave and the dead.

Did I know him in life? Yes, as brother knows brother;
  I knew him and loved him—'twas all I could give,
My love. 'But the fact is we loved one another,
  And either would die that the other might live.
Rough in his ways? Yes; but kind and good-hearted;
  There wasn't a flaw in the heart of Wild Bill,
And well I remember the day that we started
            That grave on the hill.

A good scout? I reckon there wasn't his equal,
  Both Fremont and Custer could vouch for that fact.
Quick as chain-lightning with rifle or pistol—
  And this is what Custer said—" Bill never backed."
He called me his " kid "—I was only a boy;
  And to ungratefulness Bill was a stranger,
Ready to share every sorrow and joy,
            Brave hunger and danger.

And now let me show you the good that was in him—
  The letters he wrote to his Agnes—his wife;
Why, a look or a smile, one kind word could win him.
  Hear part of this letter—the last of his life:

" AGNES DARLING: If such should be that we never meet again, while firing
my last shot I will gently breathe the name of my wife—my Agnes—and with a
kind wish even for my enemies, I will make the plunge and try to swim to the
other shore."

Oh, Charity! come fling your mantle about him;
  Judge him not harshly—he sleeps 'neath the sod.
Custer—brave Custer!—was lonely without him,
            Even with God.

Charge, comrades, charge! see young Custer ahead!
  His charger leaps forth, almost flying;
One volley! and half of his comrades are dead—
  The other half fighting and dying!
Let us hope, while their dust is reposing beneath
  The dirge-singing pines in the mountains,
That Christ has crowned each with an evergreen wreath,
  And given them to drink from His fountains.

CUSTER'S LAST CHARGE.

(Taken from "Tic Tacs," by permission of Homer Lee Bank-Note Co.)

"HE DIED FOR ME."

(As told to me by a veteran scout in the graveyard of a frontier military post.)

I TELL ye, pard, in this Western wild
As a gineral thing the dirt's jist piled
In a rather permiscuous sort o' way
On top of a private soldier's clay ;
An' one'd think from the marble shaft,
An' the flowers a-wavin' above the graft,
That a major-gineral holds that tomb ;
But the corpse down thar wore a private's plume.

I remember the day they swore Mead in ;
He war' pale-complected an' rather thin ;
He'd bin w'at they call a trampin' beat,
An' enlisted fur want o' somethin' to eat.
It's allus the case that a new recruit
Is the butt o' tricks from the older fruit ;
An' the way the boys tormented the cuss
War' real down wicked an' scandalous.

He tuk it all with a sickly smile,
An' said if they'd wait till arter awhile,
When he got fed up in some sort o' trim,
It moughtn't be healthy to fool with him.
An' I knowed by the look o' the feller's eye—
Fur all he war' back'ard an' rather shy—
That behind his skeleton sort o' breast
A heart like a lion's found a nest.

One night as the guard at twelve o'clock
Relieved the sentinel over the stock,
The corporal seed a sort of a glare
From toward the officers' quarters there.
The alarm was raised an' the big gun fired,
An' the soldiers, not more'n half attired,
Cum rushin' out on the barrack ground,
With a wild an' excited sort o' bound.

The commander's quarters war' all afire,
An' the flames a-mountin' higher an' higher,
An' what with the yells o' men, an' the shrieks
O' the officers' wives, with whitish cheeks,
An' the roar o' the flames, an' devilish light
Illuminatin' the pitch-dark night,
'Twar' sich a sight as I've of'en thought
You could see in hell w'en it's bilin' hot!

An' then with a wild, despairin' yell
The commander shouted, "My God, where's Nell?"
His wife responded, "She's in her bed!'
Then fell to the ground like a person dead.
Up through the roof the mad flames roared,
An' the blindin' smoke in a dense mass poured
Through every crevice an' crack, till a cloud
Hung above like a death-black funeral shroud.

(It mightn't be out o' place to state,
As kinder accountin' fur this Mead's fate,
That Nell war' an angel, ten year old,
With a heart as pure as the virgin gold,
An' she had a kind of an angel trick
Of readin' an' sich like to the sick;
An' many's the dainty her hands 'd bear
To Mead w'en he lay in the hospital there.)

My God! It war' 'nuff to raise the hair
On the head of a marble statue: there
Stood a crowd of at least two hundred men,
None darin' to enter that fiery pen—
Men that war' brave on an Injun trail,
Whose courage war' never known to fail;
But to enter that buildin' was certain death,
So they stood thar' starin', and held their breath.

Then all at once, with an eager cry
An' a bulldog look in his flashin' eye,
This Mead rushed up to the wailin' band,
An' a paper thrust in the colonel's hand;

" My mother's address," he said, an' then
He sort o' smiled on the crowd o' men,
An', jist like a flash o' lightnin', shot
Through the door right inter the seethin' pot.

With a yell of horror the crowd looked on,
Fur they thought with him it war' good-by, John ;
But a half a minute after the dash
An up-stairs winder burst with a crash,
An' thar' stood Mead like a smilin' saint,
The gal in his arms in a deathlike faint,
An' he yelled fur a rope, an' let 'er down
To terry firmy (w'ich means the groun').

Then he tied the rope to the winder sash
Fur to foller down, but thar' cum a crash,
An' the blazin' roof, with a fearful din,
Throwed the boy to the groun' as it tumbled in !
We carried him 'way from the fearful heat,
A-hopin' the noble heart still beat :
But the old post surgeon shook his head,
An' said with a sigh that Mead war' dead !

     *   *   *   *   *

'T'wan't very long afore little Nell
Got over the shock, an' as soon as well
She circulated among the men,
With a sheet o' paper, an' ink, an' pen,
An' axed each one fur to give his mite
In remembrance o' Mead's brave work that night;
An' as the result this monument stands,
'Mid flowers planted by Nell's own hands.

An' every evenin' she walks up here,
The boys all think fur to drop a tear;
An' I've seed her, too, on her knees right there,
With her face turned up'ards, as if in prayer.
You'll see, that line at the top's to tell
As how the stone war' " ERECTED BY NELL,"
An' down at the bottom thar' you'll see
Some Bible readin'—" HE DIED FOR ME."

A MOUNTAIN GIRL'S LETTER.

DEAR Tobe, since you left for the mountains
   Old Nick has broke loose on the ranch,
And that's why I've squatted to write you
   The news of the last avalanche.
For I'm yours—and I'm yours with a vengeance—
   And I don't give a snap for the gang,
Since we plighted our love to each other
   In the wild mountain song that we sang.

So Tobe, dear old boy, don't you worry,
   No matter what this may disclose,
While I look at the flower you left me,
   And you take a peep at the rose.
Tho' faded and dead, they remind us
   Of the evening we parted last fall ;
You whispered, " My wild rose, God bless you !"
   And I—well, I blubbered—that's all.

And now, while I sit in the arbor,
   The spot where our lips snapped apart—
I felt just the same as that evening
   When my throat was chock-full of my heart.
The lump has gone down, but I'd rather
   Be choked half to death with you here
Than swim in a tank of co-log-ney,
   When you, my own boy, wasn't near.

Well, you know, Tobe, before we got spooney
   (Of course you remember all that),
And the rooster who wore the eye-glasses
   And the two-and-a-half-story hat ;
And you know how I hated the donkey,
   With his fine hair and screwed-up mustache ;
But, Lord ! how he monkeyed around me,
   While up to my elbows in wash.

And, Tobe, you'd a busted your waist-band
 If you'd seen me a-splashin' the suds,
While the bubbles just sacheyed around him
 And dropped on his dudey-like duds.
And dad, he was watchin' my capers,
 And soon as the dandy vamoused
I felt kinder skeered fur a minnit,
 And wished I could fly to your roost.

You know the old folks often told me
 My face was a fortune itself ;
They didn't like you worth a copper,
 And wanted you laid on the shelf.
They tried to kick up sich a racket,
 And swore they would keep us apart,
But, golly, in spite of the kickin',
 You just waltzed away with my heart.

But, pshaw ! you had hardly got started
 When the no-account snob ambled 'round ;
Oh, jimminy, wasn't he lovin',
 And didn't he look like a hound !
As thin as a coyote, and skinny,
 And sportin' a button bokay—
A regular poor piece of " croppin "
 That old Satan could skeersely assay.

And then he begun his soft nonsense.
 And said how he come from " the Hub."
Said I, " If you don't leave the parlor
 My sweetheart will draw to a club."
Which, he said, kinder mixed him a little,
 And he didn't just quite understand,
So I showed him a flush, and I whispered
 That you held a pretty good hand.

But, jokin' aside, boy, he's wealthy,
 Owns stock in the big Torrence mine,
Drives a fine pair of A 1 Comanches,
 And I reckon he works the best wine.

But, you see, he got thick with the old 'uns,
   And wanted to marry me here,
But you bet that I busted that racket,
   And kicked like a two-year-old steer.

I jest made him waltz to my music,
   And, make no mistake, it was real ;
I borrowed that little self-cocker,
   So often discharged by young Teal.
I knew it would cause a sensation
   In the house of old Buckshot McGee,
But somebody promised Tobias,
   And, don't you forget it, that's we.

But now comes the worst of the racket,
   I'm in for a long, weary day,
I'm locked in the room near the attic,
   And I reckon the devil's to pay ;
'Cause I whispered to father and mother
   That their dandy I never would wed,
And that's why I borrowed Teal's whistler,
   To blow off the top of his head.

That's why I'm shut up in my chamber,
   But, Tobies dear, that's nothing new,
For many's the night, my old fellow,
   Have I not been shut up with you.
That is, in my dreams I have been there,
   So, Tobe, I must go to my bed,
And I'll never say yes to the dandy,
   Nor go back on a word I have said.

So be easy, you dear, good old miner,
   Till I meet you again by the well,
And I'll marry my Tobe, the old-timer,
   And that's what's the matter with
                  NELL.

TO MRS. I. P. JENKS.

(Written in her scrap-book on her wedding day, April 16, 1884.)

THE marriage bells have just ceased ringing,
   And you have ceased to be a maid ;
And little birds are sweetly singing
   For you and Ike a serenade.
All Nature seems to smile serenely,
   The sunbeams kiss the budding rose,
While Ike exclaims : " Ye gods, how queenly !"
   As inward love's pure streamlet flows.

And oh ! I pray that love unceasing,
   Pure and holy, shall prevail,
Year by year its strength increasing,
   As you journey on life's trail.
Cloudless skies and sunny weather,
   Roses budding on the way ;
Hand in hand through life together—
   Heart-strings tuned in love's sweet lay.

And to Ike, my boy pard, the following impromptu lines are affectionately
inscribed :

MEMORIES.

PARTNER of my boyhood days,
   When hearts were young and wild,
Companion of my wicked ways,
When up the hills and down the braes
The farmer stood in perfect maze ;
   I'll draw the picture mild !

The farmer stood—the dog did not :
   We ran o'er fields and ditches ;
To-day, methinks, I see the spot,
And you could point it out, I wot,
That fence whereon the bulldog got
   The half-sole of your breeches.

And as these scenes come back anew
  I see again my father's frown,
And while the switch was hard on you,
To me the club was nothing new ;
For weeks I had to twist and screw—
  It hurt me to sit down.

But ours was not a safe retreat,
  And soon we left the old home nest,
And trudged along with weary feet,
In rain and storm, in snow and sleet,
And for a crust of bread to eat
  With saw-buck did we wrest.

And then it was our mother's voice
  Would wake us from our dreams—
We chose, " because we had no choice,"
To make our mothers' heart rejoice—
And soon their wicked wayward boys
  Pulled back against the stream.

And so, boy pard, we've stemmed the tide,
  Tho' few the laurels won,
And you are happy with your bride,
While mine is smiling by my side.
God grant no evil may betide
  Till God shall say, " Well done."

And then, if up the golden tree
  Successfully we climb.
Our angel mothers we shall see,
And boys who fought with you and me
To make God's flag and country free :
  Ah ! that will be sublime.

              Your boy pard,
                  " CAPTAIN JACK."

SOMEBODY.

Oh, would I were somebody's darling,
　　And somebody cared for me,
And that I was loved by somebody,
　　And somebody sat on my knee.
And then perhaps that somebody
　　Would be somebody very dear,
And life would be blessed with somebody,
　　And somebody make it less drear.

Alas! I *was* loved by somebody,
　　And somebody kissed my brow,
And I smiled when a boy on somebody,
　　And somebody smiles on me now.
That dear, sweet face of somebody,
　　Of somebody true and brave,
The sunburst of hope for somebody
　　That laid her away in the grave.

And the angel face of somebody
　　Seems watching over me still.
And though I weep for somebody,
　　As I journey over life's hill,
I know I am loved by somebody,
　　And somebody wishes me joy,
For I had a love for somebody,
　　That somebody had for her boy.

She is there with the angels, somebody,
　　Who watched over me when a child,
An angel on earth was somebody,
　　When I was youthful and wild.
But God had called for somebody,
　　And somebody's work is done,
And somebody waits with the angels,
　　To welcome her wayward son.

THE BURIAL OF WILD BILL.

(To Charley Utter—Colorado Charley.)

UNDER the sod in the prairie-land
  We have laid him down to rest,
With many a tear from the sad, rough throng
  And the friends he loved the best ;
And many a heartfelt sigh was heard
  As over the earth we trod,
And many an eye was filled with tears
  As we covered him with the sod.

Under the sod in the prairie-land
  We have laid the good and the true—
An honest heart and a noble scout
  Has bade us a last adieu.

No more his silvery laugh will ring,
   His spirit has gone to God ;
Around his faults let Charity cling
   While you cover him with the sod.

Under the sod in the land of gold
   We have laid the fearless Bill ;
We called him Wild, yet a little child
   Could bend his iron will.
With generous heart he freely gave
   To the poorly clad, unshod—
Think of it, pards—of his noble traits—
   While you cover him with the sod

Under the sod in Deadwood Gulch
   You have laid his last remains ;
No more his manly form will hail
   The red man on the plains.
And, Charley, may Heaven bless you !
   You gave him a " bully good send ;"
Bill was a friend to you, pard,
   And you were his last, best friend.

You buried him 'neath the old pine tree,
   In that little world of ours,
His trusty rifle by his side—
   His grave all strewn with flowers ;
His manly form in sweet repose,
   That lovely silken hair—
I tell you, pard, it was a sight,
   That face so white and fair !

And while he sleeps beneath the sod
   His murderer goes free,*
Released by a perjured, gaming set,
   Who'd murder you and me—

* Tried and released by a lot of petty gamblers, but afterward arrested at Laramie City, and taken to Yankton, Dakota, tried and hung.

Whose coward hearts dare never meet
　　A brave man on the square.
Well, pard, they'll find a warmer clime
　　Than they ever found out there.

Hell is full of just such men ;
　　And if Bill is above to-day,
The Almighty will have enough to do
　　To keep him from going away—
That is, from making a little scout
　　To the murderers' home below ;
And if old Peter will let him out,
　　He can clean out the ranch, I know.

I'M SAD TO-NIGHT.

Lines suggested by the following remark from a young lady at a Christmas
party : " Captain, you seem happy always."

I'm sad to-night, and yet my face
　　Is only marked with cunning smiles,
For looking in the glass I trace
　　In every feature false beguiles.

I'm sad to-night, and yet they say,
　　Because I dance and laugh and sing,
That I am always, oh ! so gay,
　　And laugh with such a merry ring.

But I would scorn to show my grief,
　　I use my muscle and my brain ;
For work will always bring relief,
　　And sunshine comes just after rain.

And though the game is hard to find,
　　I have no time to weep or wail ;
Let those who will remain behind,
　　I'll still pursue the same old trail.

I'm sad to-night, and yet just now
　　A hundred merry voices rang ;
There's perspiration on each brow,
　　From laughing at the song I sang.

I'm sad to-night—why do I sing?
　　Because God gave me voice and power !
And oft I've made the woodland ring,
　　While all alone with some wild flower.

And often on the lonely trail
　　I've bursted out with something new ;
I started with a song from Yale,
　　I'm singing yet in Cariboo.

I'm sad to-night, and yet should I
　　Let others know one care or sorrow,
While hope is whispering by-and-by ?
　　No ! no ! 'twill be all right to-morrow.

I'm sad to-night, but sweet ambition
　　Tells me that I must hold my own ;
And while lasts the ammunition
　　I will hold the fort alone.

For other skies have clouded o'er me,
　　And other moons have shown less bright,
But thou, fair star of hope before me,
　　Hath always been my beacon light.

And so I'll tarry with thee longer,
　*　Ever faithful, firm and true,
With confidence still growing stronger,
　　In thy high hills, fair Cariboo !

And I believe with those old-timers
　　That there is luck for thee and thine—
Lucky years for all our miners,
　　Forty, Sixty, Seventy-nine.

NATURE'S TREASURES.

DEEP within her breast doth Nature hide
   Her precious ores—her silver and her gold,
While rough, uncouth upon the mountain-side,
   Is found the tempting float—a tale untold.
The hardy pioneer with eager eye
   Scans every boulder with a wistful glance,
And tho' a hundred times he fail, will try
   Another trip—there's still another chance.

With hopeful heart in Nature's solitude,
   He prospects hill and gulch, and every night
In his abode uncouth perchance and rude,
   He dreams of home and wife, and prospects bright.
And time rolls on, his form is bending low,
   The fire has gone from out those bright blue eyes,
His chestnut hair has turned as white as snow,
   And yet, half blind, he finds a wealthy prize.

And what is wealth or what is influence
   If life has scarce an hour for happy thought?
Would Nature's vaults disclosed half recompense
   The ravages that care and toil have wrought?
The miner leaves his happy home and wife
   To share his love with fashion's yellow god,
And some I've known, and shared their toil and strife,
   In Chloride, now lie sleeping 'neath the sod.

They came for gold, but those were early days,
   When beasts of prey, in shape of fiends, ran wild:
When "noble reds" were sung in minstrel lays,
   And none were noble save the prairie child.
Oh! Mother Nature, if thou didst conceive
   And bear such offering as they claim for you,
Disclose thy treasure-vaults, and while you grieve
   Thy breast will soften with thy tears of dew.

Oh ! if we only knew, and knowing cared,
    To share those precious gems in Nature's breast,
The child of want and woe would then be reared
    In love and peace, and none would be distressed.
But not until her breast is torn apart
    With cruel blows and giant's powerful blast
Will she disclose the secrets of her breast,
    And then monopoly will'hold them fast.

A curse be on the men who hoard their stores
    While want and woe and heavy hearts repine,
And begging but a crust at their back doors,
    Hear sounds of revelry and popping wine ;
But ignorance is bliss, and these poor souls,
    Deformities of want and woe and shame,
In blissful ignorance and flowing bowls
    Attempt to drown their sorrows—who's to blame ?

God knows I speak the truth when I declare
    I would not change my heart for wealth of Gould ;
For if I tried to climb the golden stair,
    Some honest soul would tell me I was fool'd.
If God is good, and surely He must be,
    I'll take my chances with the poor and meek ;
And if our hills will share their wealth with me,
    I'll fight monopoly—and assist the weak.

And if when all earth's weary work for me
    Is ended, and I lay me down to die,
A thousand careworn faces I shall see
    Made happy when they come to say good-by,
And then if up the golden stair I climb,
    When Gabriel toots I'll whisper through his tin
I scattered gold and sunshine down below,
    St. Peter sure will bid me waltz right in.

MY MOUNTAIN HOME.

FAR beyond the rolling prairie
  Is a home more dear to me
Than your grand and stately mansions,
  Or your cottage by the sea ;
In a little dell that's girdled
  By the mountains, rocks and trees,
And the notes of Nature's songsters
  Making music in the breeze.

Why I love my shady woodland,
  Why I love each flowery dell,
Where, beside my trusty comrades,
  I have fought where many fell ;
Where so oft alone I've wandered,
  Sat and mused the whole day long,
To the music of the songsters
  I have sang my humble song.

It is grand in Nature's grandeur,
  Thus to live and love as well,
Where around the blazing camp-fire
  Stories we would hear and tell,
And, with merry voices ringing,
  Comrades joined me in my rhymes,
While we sang of by-gone pleasures
  And the days of other times.

Oh, how happy in the woodland,
  Or beside some mountain brook,
Where so oft the speckled beauties
  Dangled shining on my hook ;
Where the deer and elk were grazing,
  Where the buffalo loved to stray,
Birds on every sheet of water,
  And life seemed a long day's play.

Then at night, when all was quiet,
  How my friends would gather near,
In the little old log cabin,
  Where each hardy pioneer
Used to laugh and shout so hearty
  To the banjo's merry tone—
Shall we meet no more, dear comrades,
  In that little mountain home?

SPRING IN THE BLACK HILLS.

BEAUTIFUL Spring in the highlands of nature,
  Snow on the hill-tops and grass in the vale ;
Sunshine is beaming on each living creature,
  And not e'en one sorrow our joys to assail.
The pine trees are bowing and bending before us,
  The miner is building his new cabin home ;
And the birds seem to carol in musical chorus,
  " Angels watch o'er you where'er you may roam."

Beautiful Spring, you will loosen the fountains,
  Long sealed by the frost in the valleys and hills ;
And down from the tops of the mightiest mountains
  Will dance little streamlets and murmuring rills.
Blessings will follow—we feel it, believe it—
  If men will be faithful and work hand in hand,
Though many will tempt you, while working, to leave it,
  But don't you be fooled, for there's gold in this land.

Beautiful Spring, you will bring us sweet flowers ;
  Thousands will gather from far o'er the land,
And many will find bright homes in these bowers,
  And, seeing the grandeur, themselves grow more grand.
Farmers will come with their ploughs and their harrows,
  The bright golden grain will be waving ere long ;
While civilization will bury the arrows,
  And the red man will sing his last sad death-song.

THE WELCOME HOME.

HOME again !   Each stalwart comrade
   Breathes his honest welcome back.
" Dog my cats, we's glad to see you,
   Laws-ee.   Whar ye bin to, Jack?
Why, old pard, we've bin a-thinkin',
   Somehow, ye had lost yer ha'r,
An' you bet yer life, we missed ye
   At our meetin's over thar."

Not one buckskin boy among them—
   Not a man in all that throng—
But was glad to gaze upon me,
   I had been away so long.
How my heart, with fond emotion,
   Beat that night at Modie's store,
When the boys, with pure devotion,
   Gathered round their chief once more !

There was Bob and Jule and Franklin,
   Bill and California Joe—
Every man an Indian fighter,
   Knowing all a scout should know.
But my songs and acts had won them,
   And amid their merry shouts,
In the Buffalo Gap entrenchments,
   I was hailed their chief of scouts.

Whether in the year succeeding
   I deserved the name or not,
By our pioneers and miners
   I shall never be forgot.
Never did the wily redskin
   Find me napping by the way,
And I tried to do my duty
   In the camp or in the fray.

CUSTER CITY, D. T.

HOOD'S CHILDREN.

[San Francisco *Post.*]

When the ex-Confederate General Hood and his wife died at New Orleans, from yellow fever, leaving nine children, the members of the Grand Army throughout the United States were the first to tender benefits and organize fairs for their relief. Lincoln Post, of San Francisco, procured the Baldwin Theatre for one night, and the entire company, including James O'Neill, Lewis Morrison, C. B. Bishop, and others volunteered, as did also T. W. Keene, then leading man at the California Theatre. On the afternoon of the day preceding the entertainment, Colonels Lyon, C. Mason Kinne, of Lincoln Post, G. A. R., and Fleurnoy, of Texas, an ex-Confederate, waited upon Captain Jack Crawford, and requested him to write a poem appropriate for the occasion; and "Remember, Jack," said Colonel Fleurnoy, "that we-uns as did the fightin' have nothin' agin you-uns as lit us." "Wal," said Jack, in that peculiar vernacular of the West and South, "I reckon, pard, as how I are right smart posted as to that," and with an "Adios, comrades—I'll try," went immediately to his room. On the next night, Col. Kinne announced that Captain Jack Crawford was to read a poem. T. W. Keene, to-day's greatest young tragedian, held Jack's manuscript, and actually pushed him before the curtain. Jack, with voice trembling with fear and emotion, stood before the grandest audience that ever sat in the Baldwin, while in the front orchestra seats sat the Blue and the Gray in uniform, above them hanging a silk banner of blue and gray, and intertwined with the Stars and Stripes, on which was inscribed: "*The Blue and the Gray under one Flag.*" Jack was dressed in his field buckskin suit; and looking all over the great mass of humanity in the galleries and below, his eyes resting on the Blue and the Gray, he began:

"My comrades in Blue, my brothers in Gray, your committee waited upon me yesterday and requested me to write something worthy of this occasion. I submit the following impromptu verses in Fraternity, Charity, and Loyalty:

"DEAR comrades and friends in the golden land,
   You may say I'm rough, you may call me wild,
But I've got a heart and a willing hand
   To feel and to work for a soldier's child.
Do you think I ask on which side *he* fought?
   If man and soldier, his record was good ;
For though our Union was dearly bought,
   All hatred is buried with Hooker and Hood.

" And, comrades, I'll tell you right here, to-night,
  The men most bitter against the Gray
Are those who never were seen in a fight,
  But who always got sick on a fighting day.
With soldiers, my friends, it is not so :
  They respect each other, the Gray and the Blue ;
Nor are they ashamed that the world shall know
  How they stood by their colors, brave men and true.

" Was Jackson ashamed when he knelt to pray
  For the cause which he thought before Heaven was just,
While marching his half-starved boys in Gray,
  On an ear of corn and a single crust?
Was Lee ashamed when he tendered his sword
  To Grant, who refused the warrior's steel?
Who said, ' Your horses shall be restored,
  For braver never wore spurs to his heel.'

" Oh ! generous hearts, in the Golden State
  You are forging the links of a Union chain,
That cables one end at the Golden Gate,
  That will circle the States to the Gulf-swept main.
A chain that will bind us, the Blue and the Gray,
  In a union of purpose the gods will approve,
In love that grows strong in adversity's day,
  And hearts that will stand by the flag that we love.

" The past—it is dead ! But we cannot forget it,
  And, comrades, we wouldn't forget if we could ;
As for myself, I shall never regret it,
  This poor little service I render for Hood.
His loved ones will not be distressed nor discarded,
  And to-night I am proud of a share in the stock,
And shall feel, as a soldier, I'm fully rewarded
  By one little prayer from his innocent flock.

" One little prayer from the loved ones we foster,
  His latest bequest to his comrades in peace,
As the pale hand of death wrote his name on the roster
  And the angel on guard gave his spirit release.

"Oh, comrades, let charity's mantle enfold them,
  Old Abe had no malice, no hate in his soul ;
On the ramparts above may we hope to behold them,
  While Washington musters each name on the roll."

SOME DAY.

TO JIM.

SOME day—I cannot tell just now,
  But hope and faith are strong,
And I can see one little ray
  Of sunshine through my song ;
And clouds that overhung my sky
  And part obscure it still,
Will leave bright sunshine by and by,
  While climbing up life's hill.

Some day—my soul inspires the thought
  That makes my path more clear.
I see one sweet forget-me-not,
  Where all was dark and drear.
And slowly on *Miss Fortune's trail*
  With eager feet I'll press,
My motto—no such word as fail,
  While courting *Miss Success.*

Some day, while kneeling at her feet
  Or sporting by her side,
I'll steal into her heart's retreat
  And claim her for my bride.
And while I hold her in my arms,
  If you should come my way,
I'll let you gaze on all her charms
  And win her too—*some day.*

ONLY A MINER KILLED.

Although everything that science, skill, and money can devise is done to avert accidents, the average of fatal ones in the Comstock is three a week. "Three men a week."

Only a miner killed ;
  Oh ! is that all ?
One of the timbers caved ;
  Great was the fall,
Crushing another one
  Shaped like his God.
Only a miner lad—
  Under the sod.

Only a miner killed,
  Just one more dead.
Who will provide for them—
  Who earn their bread ?
Wife and the little ones,
  Pity them, God,
Their earthly father
  Is under the sod.

Only a miner killed,
  Dead on the spot.
Poor hearts are breaking
  In yon little cot.
He died at his post,
  A hero as brave
As any who sleep
  In a marble-top grave.

Only a miner killed !
  God, if thou wilt,
Just introduce him
  To old Vanderbilt,
Who, with his millions,
  If he is there,
Can't buy one interest—
  Even one share.

Only a miner killed !
Bury him quick,
Just write his name on
A piece of a stick,
No matter how humble
Or plain be the grave,
Beyond all are equal—
The master and slave.

WE MEET AGAIN.

The following, written by Jim Carlin while editing a New Mexico paper, explains itself :

"Once upon a time, as the story writers say, when the hostile Indians were endeavoring to fill a contract to paint the whole western country a bright red, the writer was serving the Government in a meek and unobtrusive manner, his duties being to monkey around in advance of the troops and take observations from the back of a broncho of humble birth and modest demeanor. He never used a pack animal to carry the scalps secured, and never marred the stock of his Sharps rifle with something like 75,829 notches, each notch representing an increase in the aboriginal cemetery, but worked as faithfully as he could for $8 a day and found. While engaged in this innocent pastime he first struck the trail of Jack Crawford, who was running an opposition shop in the same line of business, and in the same territory, and the friendship there formed and cemented by the dangers which surrounded the two men has grown brighter and stronger as the years rolled by.

"When a cessation of hostilities rendered that peculiar line of business too dull to interest an adventurous nature, Jack took a little whirl at the show business with Bill Cody, and his 'pardner' of the trail and the camp-fire went back East, intending to join the church, go into the retail family grocery business and get rich. Occasional letters passed between the old friends, and they gradually drifted apart, until they entirely lost track of each other. For over five years we heard not a word from Jack, and began to fear he had got religion and had had his hair shingled The zigzag cantering along of events brought the writer to New Mexico, and a few days since he learned that his old friend of the long ago was at Fort Craig. He at once wrote to the old boy, and in response, on Tuesday last, received the following, which gave his heart a pretty severe attack of the mumps. The letter opens just as it is here given, and is a pretty good indication of the paralyzing astonishment the 'Poet Scout' felt at hearing from one whom he thought might be dead and trying to learn to play a golden harp in the angelic orchestra above:

LORD BLESS YOU, OLD PARD, SHAKE!!!

" 'Let my heart speak out in a simple song,
   To the echo of days long ago ;
Let my soul burst forth in a friendship strong,
   That grows stronger as older I grow.
For many a night when I laid me down,
   With the star-spangled heavens above me,
I thought of a friend in a far-away town
   Whom I loved, and I knew that he loved me.

" 'And I dreamed, oh ! how oft, on the lonely trail,
   When nature was hushed all around me,
That your rifle came down, when the foe would assail,
   And when enemies tried to confound me ;
And a little bird whispered, when I was awake,
   " Your pard has been dreaming about you—"
God bless you, old boy, again let us shake,
   My muse has been lonely without you.

" 'So to-night I am happy, and that's why I sing—
   Do you catch the old strain of the mountains,
When my voice, like a bird, made the old woods ring,
   In chorus with streamlets and fountains ?
When the antelope stood, and the prairie wolf stared,
   And the jack-rabbit failed e'en to start !
For they knew by my singing that peace was declared,
   As the songs welled right up from my heart.

" 'And that's how I am feeling to-night, dear old Jim,
   Though unhappy a short hour ago ;
But while reading your letter my eyesight was dim,
   Though my eyes have not failed me, I know—

" ' But a something came up in my throat, dear old boy,
    That I've not felt before for a year ;
But, Jimmy, I swallowed the big lump of joy,
    And I just washed it down with a tear.' "

———

MY LITTLE NEW LOG CABIN IN THE HILLS.

A PARODY.

Written at Custer City, in the Black Hills, in the spring of 1876, for Dick
Brown, the banjo-player, and sung by Dick and I, the miners joining in the
chorus, in the camp and the cabin.

In my little new log cabin home my heart is light and free,
    While the boys around me gather every day,
And the sweetest hours I ever knew are those I'm passing now,
    While the banjo makes sweet music to my lay.

Chorus.

    The scenes are changing every day, the snow is nearly gone,
        And there's music in the laughter of the rills ;
    But the dearest spot of all I know is where I love to dwell,
        In my little new log cabin in the hills.

While the birds are sweetly singing to the coming of the spring,
    And the flow'rets peep their heads from out the sod,
We feel as gay and happy as the songsters on the wing
    Who are sending up sweet anthems to their God.

                                        Chorus.

Then let us work with heart and hand, and help each other through
    In this pretty little world we call our own,
Whether building or prospecting—yes, or fighting with the Sioux,
    For 'tis hard sometimes to play your hand alone.

                                        Chorus.

FAREWELL, OLD CABIN HOME.

Ye folks of fashion and renown,
Who live in city and in town,
And who, 'mid luxury and ease,
Have everything the heart to please,
And every morning take your ride,
'Mid worldly pomp and fashion's pride,
At evening down the promenade
With lovely girls and hearts all glad,
And home—ah! that must be divine—
A little moss-grown hut is mine.

Where the streamlet's merry lay
    Makes sweet music with its laughter,
Dancing, rippling day by day—
    I shall hear it ever after.

Where, from Harney's snow-clad crown,
Many rills come dancing down,
Where the speckled beauties glide
Swiftly through the silvery tide,
You may have your stall-fed steers—
I have lots of mountain deers.
You may have your hot-house greens,
I the good old standard beans—
Beans and pork.   Sometimes he'd kill
A buffalo bull, would Buffalo Bill;
Then with chicken, grouse and quail,
And splendid soup from buffalo tail.

Oh, how happy, gay and free
    O'er the mountains wild I roam—
Bank stocks never trouble me
    In my little mountain home.

Up the mountain, down the glen—
Dangerous? Only now and then.
If a bear you want to court,
Take her where the hair is short;

If you want a fond embrace,
Meet old Bruin face to face.
If she's strong, with frame well knit,
You'll find her most affectionate.

Bears and buffaloes, what care I—
    Catermounts may rave and foam ;
I must leave you by and by,
    So farewell, old cabin home.

Nature grand and wild and free,
Full of life and ecstasy ;
Courting nature, dead in love,
Coo again, thou gentle dove ;
Teach me, bird of paradise,
How to thaw the lover's ice ;
Make the blood within me boil—
Man must love, or man must spoil ;
Tell me, how am I to love,
And a maiden's fancy move ?

Will you miss me when I go—
   When away from you I roam ?
If your nest should fill with snow
   You can take my cabin home.

Good-by, scenes of mountain bliss,
Where the clouds come down to kiss
Crowning rocks and hiding trees,
Until lifted with the breeze.
Farewell, valley of my heart !
Time has come when we must part ;
Farewell, all thy sweet wild flowers !
All thy nooks and shady bowers—
Nevermore my eyes can see
Valley half so fair as thee.

Valley, cabin, all farewell !
   Oh, for one forget-me-not !
I would leave it in the dell—
   Plant it near this moss-grown cot.

CASTLE CREEK, BLACK HILLS.

IT'S ONLY A DIME.

The following letter, inclosing a silver dime, was received at the Mayor's office:

NEW YORK, July 30.

" MR. MAYOR : I see a orphan sojer's boy sends five cents, and calls it his mite ; I send ten. My dad was a sojer, and they say he was a good one. He was with Grant, and I guess he is now. I sell papers and black boots. If Vanderbilt and Gould and dem oder big fellows give as much as they could afford, same as me and the oder boys, General Grant's monument would be bigger than the staty of Liberty.   JOHNNY.

" *Postscript.*—Mother says, Don't sine your name, cos dey mention it in the papers. Mother is a widder, and I goes to Sunday-school. Call this Johnny's mite."

While reading this, vivid memories came up before me, and I felt as if this little tribute would not be out of place :

You may talk of the love of little Nell,
  Of her wreath and her innocent bliss,
But oh ! how each comrade's heart will swell
  When he thinks of a love like this !

"It is only a dime," said the little waif ;
  But, boys, it was rich and bright.
There never was locked in a banker's safe
  Such riches as this boy's mite.

"For dad was a soldier, too," he said,
  "An' a good un, the soldiers say ;
An' dad was with Grant wherever he led,
  An' dad is with Grant to-day."

And, boys, who knows, though his dad is dead,
  This peer of your snob galoots
May be carving his way to the nation's head
  Selling papers and blacking boots.

NEW YEAR'S DAY IN THE BLACK HILLS—1876.

BEYOND the Mississippi,
  And the old Missouri, too,
On the far and distant prairie,
  With comrades brave and true,
One year ago I wandered
  In the hills so far away ;
I was happy in my cabin
  One year ago to-day.

The morning was a fair one,
  And the skies were bright and clear,
And the snow like diamonds sparkled,
  While we chased the panting deer ;
I never will forget it,
  Each miner lad felt gay,
For we found a splendid prospect
  One year ago to-day.

A band of hardy miners
  At evening gathered round,
Some on rustic benches
  And others on the ground ;
We ate and drank together,
  Our hearts were light and gay,
For a Concord coach first entered
  Our Hills last New Year's day.

And as the noble horses
  Came flying up the street,
With fifteen hardy miners,
  You bet, it was a treat ;
And the noble Colonel Patrick,
  'Twas this I heard him say :
'Come in and take a drink, boys,
  For this is New Year's day.''

But time has worked its wonders,
  And in every gulch and glen,
Instead of half a hundred,
  Ten thousand hardy men,
With sluice and pan and rocker,
  Work hard and trust in heaven ;
And twenty Concord coaches
  Are there in Seventy-seven.

THE RUINED VIRGINIA.

(Virginia City, Nevada, almost totally destroyed by fire, October, 1876.)

DID I hear the news from Virginny,
  The news of that terrible fire ?
Yes ; but I couldn't believe it
  When it first came over the wire ;
But when I found it square, pard,
  I weakened, you bet, right here,
And I didn't care a tinker's
  Who saw me drop a tear.

Just reason the thing for a minute—
  There's two thousand miners right there,
It's cold, way up in the mountains,
  And some's got no breeches to wear.
And that ain't the worst ; for instance,
  There's two of my old pards hurt,
And a dozen that wore plugs Sunday
  Ain't got the first stitch but their shirt.

Now, Jack, ain't that rough on Virginny ?
  Well, there ain't no saints out there ;
And I 'spec' it's a second Chicago,
  And this is a kind of a scare.

But dog my cats if I see it
    Exactly in that thar way,
For most of them hardy miners
    Are honest, by Joe, as the day.

But maybe it's all for the better—
    That's what the good people say ;
But I don't want any in mine, pard,
    If the Lord will but keep it away.
I don't read much in the Scripture,
    But I've heard the good parson talk
About sinners bein' punished by brimstone
    When against the commandments they balk.

Now, I don't jist understand it,
    Though I tumble to what they say ;
Nor I don't see why the Almighty
    Should treat a poor man in that way.
While the fellers who's got the lucre,
    And the worst to connive and swear,
Always give us poor devils the euchre—
    The deal ain't exactly square.

And if, as the parson tells us,
    There's a place after this, called hell,
With fire and red-hot brimstone—
    With a nasty kind of smell ;
I'll be dogged if some fine snoozers
    (That I have a reason to know)
Won't find a scorchin' old corner
    In that furnace way down below.

Now, there was old Kit McGregor,
    He was rough and ready, but smart ;
He could whip any man in the diggin's—
    And there wasn't a flaw in his heart.
But when old Parson Plum, one evening,
    Done dirt—didn't act on the square—
He sent the daylight clear through him,
    And laid the old sinner out there.

Now, is Kit goin' to hell for that, Jack?
　　Not much! the Lord bid him shoot,
And he killed a worm of the devil—
　　A hypocrite, rogue, and galoot.
Besides, the gal was his darter,
　　And she panned out a woman most fair,
And was loved by all in the diggin's—
　　But Kit had revenge right there.

IRENE IS DEAD.

The following letter, written by the noted writer of frontier tales, Ned Buntline, furnished the theme for the verses bearing the above title, and which are now published for the first time :

"EAGLE'S NEST, N. Y., Jan. 17, 1881.

"MY DEAR CRAWFORD : Three words speak the agony which volumes could not describe, the loss which all the gold in your mines could not replace, the shadow which hangs darkest in all my long, eventful life—*Irene is dead!*

"My little pet, my darling, our household angel, my only one, has taken wing for heaven. Her marble cold form sleeps beneath the snow on yonder hillside, but her spirit is in the land of eternal light and song.

"God help us! My wife's grief is crushing. I bear as bear I *must*, but no past agony ever reached this. . . .

"Give my love to your boys. You may see me in the saddle in the spring. My beautiful home is a desert to me now. Were it not for my wife, I'd be with you inside of two weeks.

　　　　　"Yours faithfully,
　　　　　　　　"E. Z. C. JUDSON (Ned Buntline)."

IN THE FIELD, OJO CALIENTE, N. M., Feb. 3, 1881.

DEAR OLD HEART : Your sorrowful yet beautifully touching letter, containing the sad news of Irene's death, is at hand, and the rough frontiersman, your friend, can only drop a silent tear ; but if you could look through the dark tangled undergrowth away into the clear sunlight of my soul, at this moment, you could witness the beating of a heart that is all sympathy for thee and thine in thy deep sorrow and bereavement. *Irene is dead!* Oh, that her gentle spirit would act as a medium to-night, that would manifest itself in poetic expression! But my hand trembles at the thought. In the midst of savages, suffering at this moment from a wound received but three days ago, and looking each day upon the new-made graves of friends and brothers, how can I, amid such scenes,

express in true poetic spirit sentiments worthy as a memoriam to this angel?
Thy only rose, thy sweet Irene. Those three words contain more than would
fill volumes—*Irene is dead!*

Irene is dead! Thine only one,
  Thy little household pet,
Transplanted from a world of sin,
  A rose in Eden set.
How sweet the thought ! why, dear old heart,
  That land is far more fair,
And Heaven decreed that you should part
  To meet again up there.

Irene is dead! Do angels die ?
  No, no ; but He doth sever
The hearts He loves—*Irene will live*,
  Forever and forever.
Bow not thy aged head in grief,
  For Irene knows no pain,
And all is love, and joy, and peace,
  Where you shall meet again.

Irene's asleep ! Thy little rose
  Has lain her down to rest ;
Her marble face in sweet repose,
  The snow above her breast ;
The pure white snow, a fitting shroud
  For thine own sweet Irene,
Whose life had never known a cloud,
  Thine own heart's fairy queen.

Thine only one hath taken wing,
  Thy little household dove !
Methinks I hear the angels sing
  In chorus, love with love,
And Irene's voice is in that throng :
  "Sweet ma and papa dear,
Your darling sings a sweeter song
  While waiting for you here."

  Fraternally yours, J. W. CRAWFORD (Captain Jack).

AMONG THE PEAKS.

Oh, gentle breeze, from sunny South,
　　With scent of fragrant flowers,
Warm again with thy heated breath
　　These sovereign hills of ours.

Burst forth in every mountain glen
　　Where streams no longer flow,
With sunny beams from azure sky,
　　To melt the crusted snow.

And onward from the boisterous sea
　　Sweep clouds of tepid rain ;
Let thunder be thy bugle call
　　To free our hills again.

And when the distant roll is heard,
　　'Twill set each heart aglow,
For many who have waited long
　　Will see our streams o'erflow.

Our hearts will greet the smiling sun,
　　And bless the heavenly rain ;
And hope, now dead, will come to life
　　When spring is here again.

And hardy, honest sons of toil
　　Will grasp their tools once more ;
Hydraulic, drift and sluice again,
　　As in the days of yore.

And when the summer time has come,
　　With hearts and mountains free,
Each day a stronger link will forge
　　To bind our harmony.

Cariboo, B. C.

FAREWELL TO OUR CHIEF.

The following lines were written on the field on the same day that Buffalo Bill bade farewell to the command, August 24th, 1876, when I was appointed to succeed him as chief of scouts.

FAREWELL! the boys will miss you, Bill ;
  In haste let me express
The deep regret we all must feel
  Since you have left our mess.
While down the Yellowstone you glide,
  Old pard, you'll find it true,
That there are thousands in the field
  Whose hearts beat warm for you.

And while we wish you every joy,
  Wherever you may roam —
Success in everything you try,
  And happiness at home ;
Yet would we wish you ever near
  To join us in the shouts
Of courage when the foe is near,
  And hail you Chief of Scouts !

So, Bill, old boy, we wish you well —
  We cannot wish you more ;
On sentiment we will not dwell —
  You've been with us before ;
Your smiling face, your manly form,
  The starlight in your eye,
In memory always will be dear —
  God bless you, pard — good-by !

DEATH OF LITTLE KIT.

(To his Father, Buffalo Bill.)

The following verses were written at Custer City, D. T., on hearing from Mr. Cody (Buffalo Bill) of the death of his little boy, Kit Carson Cody.

My friend, I feel your sorrow
  Just as though it were my own,
And I think of you each morrow
  As I ponder, when alone,
On the wonders of our Maker,
  As the world goes round and round ;
Since Kit is with his namesake
  In the happy hunting-ground.

But the parson used to tell us
  Of things we little knew,
And how the Lord would chasten
  The good, the brave and true ;
That all was for the better,
  Though it used to tax my wit,
Till I heard he sent an angel
  For your darling little Kit.

At first I thought, but thinking
  Made me wonder still the more,
Till at last I saw a vision
  While I slumbered on the floor
Of my little new log cabin
  In the Hills, not long ago.
Yes, I saw the old Kit Carson,
  With a beard as white as snow.

He wore the same old buckskin,
  But white, as if just tanned,
And beyond him, on the prairie,
  Was a scene so very grand

That I would not dare describe it—
  But that voice, that well-known sound—
The words were, " Pards, I'm happy
  In the happy hunting-ground !"

I saw an angel hover
  O'er a dark ravine below
The rippling, dancing water
  That in silvery streams did flow.
Then downward went the angel ;
  Old Kit just leaped for joy,
When from below that angel
  Brought Kit, your darling boy.

The old man raised him fondly,
  And clasped him to his breast,
While peace and sweet contentment
  Upon him seemed to rest.
Just then a painted redskin
  Was scowling from a mound,
When crack went Kit's old rifle,
  And the fiend went under ground.

And then a milk-white pony
  And a steed as white as snow,
With wide-expanded nostrils,
  Were roaming to and fro,
When Kit exclaimed, " Come, darlings,
  My prairie birds, this way !"
And soon they both were mounted,
  While the choir began to play.

I heard the sweetest music
  That mortal ever heard,
While steed and snow-white pony
  Were flying like a bird.
I woke, and in my cabin
  Your letter soon was found ;
And Kit had joined his namesake
  In the happy hunting-ground.

And, pard, when life is ended,
   If acting on the square,
We, too, will meet old Carson
   And your baby-boy up there.

UNDER THE SNOW.

IN MEMORIAM.

(Lines on the Death of T. R. Pattullo.)

UNDER the snow we have laid him down—
   Down in the depths of the grave !
The dearest, kindest heart in the camp
   Has passed o'er eternity's wave.
Gone forever ! alas, can it be,
   Will we never again see his face ?
Never again clasp his honest hand,
   With its warm and earnest embrace ?

Under the snow in the golden land,
   So far from the home of his mother,
No loving sister to close his eyes,
   But the hand of a faithful brother.
God help that mother and sister, too !
   The news will be sad we know,
" Our own dear boy in Cariboo
   Is dead and under the snow !"

" Dear mother"—and now I speak for Tom—
   "Dear mother, don't grieve for me,
I've only laid me down to rest
   Beneath the old pine tree.
So tired, dear mother, I needed rest,
   To sleep, to dream, to die ;
And God does all things for the best,
   I'll meet you by and by."

Under the snow!   The setting sun
  Seemed bathed in tears to-day,
And all are lonely in the camp
  Since Tom has passed away.
And many were the heartfelt sobs,
  And many tears did flow,
And charity round his faults we flung,
  With a mantle of pure white snow.

Under the snow he sleeps to-day,
  Mourned by the sad rough throng,
And just before he passed away
  He spoke of his favorite song,
" Maid of Athens !" beautiful maid !
  There she stands at the door !
Ere we part—another verse,
  'Twill ring on the other shore.

Under the snow the heart is still
  In death forevermore—
The heart that never saw distress
  Go hungry from his door.
And many, many will attest,
  Who left here long ago,
A truer friend than all the rest
  Now sleeps beneath the snow.

Under the snow!   A sinner sleeps—
  Real saints are very few—
But Tom was what we called a man,
  'Mongst men in Cariboo.
And when our earthly work is done
  And the world is at an end,
The Lord will not forget the man
  Who's been the poor man's friend.

THE DYING SCOUT.

(A Song to the Memory of Muggins Taylor, who was Custer's courier.)

COMRADES, raise me, I am dying,
  Hark the story I will tell ;
Break it gently to my mother,
  You were near me when I fell.
Tell her how I fought with Custer,
  How I rode to tell the news ;
Now I'm dying, comrades, dying—
  Tell me, did we whip the Sioux?

Chorus.

Comrades, raise me, I am dying,
  Catch the story I will tell ;
Break it gently to my mother,
  You were near me when I fell.

Tell my mother that, when dying,
  Every scene came back anew—
All those happy days of childhood,
  When life's cares I little knew.
Tell her that I still remember
  How she wept for very joy
When she clasped her arms around me,
  Welcomed home her soldier boy.

Chorus.

Comrades, tell my mother truly
  How we fought to hold the hill ;
Tell her how we gained the vict'ry—
  That I die a soldier still.
Hark ! I hear a voice up yonder,
  All is sunshine, bright and fair ;
Tell my mother I am dying—
  She will meet her boy up there.

Chorus.

MRS. KATE BROWNLEE SHERWOOD.

Mrs. Kate B. Sherwood, of Toledo, Ohio, is the wife of General J. R. Sherwood, Colonel of the 111th Ohio Volunteer Infantry, who won the stars of a general by gallant conduct at the battle of Franklin. She is a native Buckeye, and since her marriage, in the autumn of 1859, then in her eighteenth year, she has devoted much of her time to journalism and literature, has been a contributor to many of the leading newspapers and periodicals, editor of the Toledo *Journal* and editor of the Woman's Department of the *National Tribune*. In the spring of 1885 she published "Camp Fire and Memorial Poems," a volume of recitations for Grand Army camp fires, which has been widely read, and some of the poems have been translated into German. As an industrious literary worker she has few equals, and has translated largely from German and French into English.

It is, however, in local and State charity work that Mrs. Sherwood's character shines with its greatest lustre. In every charitable movement in her native State she has ever been a recognized leader, and was one of the original organizers of the Woman's Relief Corps, Auxiliary to the Grand Army of the Republic.

During the years 1884-85 she served as president of that organization with great honor and credit, and retired with the blessings of her co-workers and of the vast army of veterans all over the land. She is a woman of high and noble impulses, of pure Christian character, and possesses a heart which ever beats in sympathy with want and suffering, and hands ever ready to work for the unfortunate.

Just after the retirement of Mrs. Sherwood from the position of President of the Woman's Relief Corps, I had the honor to recite one of my poems in her presence, and she took her badge of office from her own bosom and pinned it to mine. This touching circumstance called forth the following:

PERHAPS.

(To Our G. A. R. Goddess—Comrade Kate B. Sherwood.)

PERHAPS, beloved goddess, you never will know it,
    The joy and the pride that inflated my soul
That night when you pinned your own badge on my bosom—
    That night when my heart wrote its name on your roll.

Perhaps it was weakness that made my eyes glisten,
    While looking in thine, rather misty, I ween,
While a warrior's soul and the heart of a woman
    Were drifting in sight of our comrade, Pauline.*

Perhaps it will be, when the moss has grown over
    A spot that is speckled with daisies just now,
Where I shall retire from life's nettles and clover,
    That I shall meet you with a crown on your brow.

Perhaps all the sunshine that dodges our coming
    Along on life's pathway will burst on to us there ;
Perhaps all the music now deaf to our thrumming
    Will thrill our tired souls in that Eden so fair.

Perhaps, after all, 'mid the strife and commotion,
    The worry and fretting of life's busy throng,
The soul will ride over the tempest-tossed ocean,
    And anchor where angels and sunshine belong.

* Paul Van Dervoort, Past Commander-in-Chief and honorary member of the Woman's Relief Corps.

Perhaps you will greet me with love, song and laughter,
  Where all our heart's yearnings will cease to exist ;
Perhaps in that wonderful, unknown hereafter,
  Our poor, weary comrades may once more enlist.

Perhaps in God's army our missing will gather,
  Unknown will be known when they answer their names ;
Not one be unseen by the all-seeing Father,
  Though sleeping in woodland, in mountain and plains.

And oh ! what an army of heroes will muster
  When Gabriel's trumpet shall call to review,
And near to the throne in a hallowed lustre
  Will stand one grand army—the Gray and the Blue.

Perhaps the great chieftains will have a reunion,
  And oh ! what a camp fire the angels will see—
Grant, Jackson and Sherman, and Hancock and Gordon,
  With Buckner and Johnston and Logan and Lee.

Perhaps each will tell of the heart's honest promptings,
  That bade them take arms on the side they thought right,
And the great Chief of all will make plain why He willed it
  Why comrades and brothers each other should fight.

Perhaps He will point to the emblem of freedom,
  As out o'er the dome her broad stripes are unfurled,
And say to those chieftains, those battle-scarred heroes,
  "Your work made that flag to enlighten the world."

And you, beloved goddess, will gather with others
  To meet them and greet them. If I can be there,
I shall ask God to let me be aide to dear mothers
  Who gave their brave sons to our country so fair.

And, Kate, if the Lord will detail me to find it,
  Your crown will be brighter than any I know ;
With sunshine in front and with starlight behind it,
  I'm sure it will light up this world here below.

SANDY'S REVENGE.

A MINER'S STRATEGY.

" I say, young feller, have something to take ?
    Yer a stranger to me, but I like yer style,
And I reckin I met ye somewhar afore—
    Come, fellers, won't ye all have a smile ?
Ye see, I've jist come in from the mines,
Where we fellers strike it rich sometimes."

" Excuse me, sir, but I never drink,
    And I'm just as much obliged to you.
I can't help it, sir, you may believe or not,
    But nevertheless I am telling you true.
And, by the way, a word in your ear—
You'll be drugged and robbed if you drink in here."

He looked at me with his great blue eyes,
    And laughingly said : " That's a very good joke.
I own a half," said he, " in the prize,"
    And looking around on the crowd as he spoke,
" I've got enough in my buckskin, I think,
To treat the house.   Come, every one, drink.

" And see here, youngster, you take a cigar.
    The other bottle—I mean the brandy.
Wall, here's how—what might be my name ?
    Wall, it might be Jim, but they call me Sandy.
And I don't know much 'bout books and sich,
But what's the odds when a feller's rich ?

" Do I want a bed ?   Wall, I reckin I do,
    And I want a good'n, ye bet yer life.
Come, set 'em up agin for the crew ;
    What's that ye say—hev I got a wife ?

Wall, now yer shouten—why, bless yer soul,
My Jennie's the trimmest gal of the whole.

"Me gettin' full? Is that what ye said?
  Wall, I reckin I am. I'll go pretty soon ;
An', landlord, when I get up to bed,
  Send me a night-cap up ter my room.
An' don't you forget it—I want it strong,
So I kin sleep on it, soundly an' long."

"Good-night !" he said, as he passed me by,
  And I saw a smile on his sunburnt face ;
And then he winked with his flashing eye,
  And whispered : " If ye kin find the place,
Jist come to my room between twelve and one,
And I reckin as how we kin have some fun."

It was nearly twelve when he said good-night,
  So I quietly left, as if to go home,
And turning quickly round to the right,
  At a corner window I saw him alone,
With a navy revolver in either hand,
He fixed them, and laid them down on the stand.

I climbed the porch ; it was rather dark,
  But somehow I managed to reach the top.
I tapped at the window and made a noise,
  When he motioned that I should stop.
Too late—the lamp was turned out quite,
And he whispered : " I'll play her alone to-night."

Five minutes ! and each to me seemed an hour,
  But at last the painful silence was broke ;
A heavy thud—then a leaden shower—
  And the little room full of fire and smoke.
A light was struck, and there on the floor
Lay landlord and son by the open door.

CHRISTMAS DAY IN THE BLACK HILLS—1876.

Last Christmas day, I remember it well—
    And I reckon I'll still remember—
When emigration began to swell,
    Though our chances war mighty slender,
A band of as bully men, by Jove,
    As ever struck out a-trailin',
Struck for the Hills ter hunt for gold,
    With bull teams just a-sailin'.

And I war guide of the outfit, pards ;
    Ye see, I'd been thar before,
When we struck it rich on Calamity Bar,
    So I struck for the Bar once more.
But I'll never forget when crossin' the Platte,
    And the ice in the middle gave way,
And down went our wagons, bulls and all—
    Pards, that war last Christmas day.

Ye see, it war only a mile across—
    Wall, that ain't much out thar—
But the boys kinder left it ter me, bein' boss,
    As ter whether the ice would bear ;
So I reckoned as how I thought it would,
    And we started—gee whoa—right away ;
But she cracked like an old cook's kettle, she did—
    Pards, that war last Christmas day.

Who cuss'd ? Oh, no, pards, I never swar,
    But just about that ar' time
There wasn't much poetry in my head—
    I couldn't a-spun a rhyme—
Ye see, the quicksands war orful bad,
    And none of us felt very gay ;
'Cause we had ter wade and carry our grub—
    Pards, that war last Christmas day.

And now while I'm ridin' on cushion seats,
  With nothin' to worry or fret,
By thunder ! I almost wish I war back
  A-courtin' my bride, my pet ;
I mean my " Winchester," bully old gal—
  And the reds will keep out of her way ;
She dropped a buck weighin' three hundred pounds—
  Pards, that war last Christmas day.

THE OLD TRAPPER'S RELIGION.

I aiN'T goin' ter preach ye a sermon,
  Nor I ain't goin' ter sing ye a song,
An' I reckin as how ye won't think so,
  If I don't draw my story too long ;
But I am jist from the church in the city,
  Whar I hear'n the good parson man tell
'Bout the psalm-singers' home up in heaven,
  An' the sinners' hot layout in hell.

I didn't at first understan' him ;
  Ye see, I sot back nigh the door,
With my leg threw way inter a tunnel,
  An' my slouch layin' flat on the floor ;
But, somehow, his words set me thinkin',
  An' it worried me ever so long,
Till I dropped on the settled conclusion
  Thet he drawed it a little too strong.

Sez he, ye must all get religion,
  An' stay with the rules o' the church,
Else, or, on the great day o' judgment
  Ye'll surely git left in the lurch.

Sez he, now's the day o' salvation,
　For why do ye weaken and wait?
Fly from that trail strew'd with pleasure,
　'Cos it leads right direct to hell's gate.

Then I ax'd myself, what is this racket
　That he seems so dead earnest about?
Is it sittin' close up near the pulpit
　To jine in the general shout?
Is it wearin' a face like a bean-pole,
　Chippin' in with a lusty amen,
An' loafin' around in the temple
　While the beggar lies sick in a pen?

Ar' these psalm-singin' nabobs religious,
　'Cause they pray in a satin-lined box,
An' all the time durin' the preachin'
　Keep plannin' their next steal in stocks?
Do ye think as they'll waltz inter glory
　Because they're mixed with the flock?
Not much!　They'll git left on the margin,
　For Christ will go down to bed rock.

In course, they're looked on as Christians,
　Tho' they gamble all week on the Board,
They freely come down with the wherewith
　To help on the cause of the Lord.
But I think at the last resurrection
　They'll have nothin' but wildcat to sell ;
And instead of the Stock Board in heaven
　They'll get points on a corner in H—ll.

Ar' the poor folks all bound to perdition
　That labor and toil day by day
For yer gilt-edged Sunday professors—
　Like Duncan*—on starvation pay?

---

* J. C. Duncan, manager of the Pioneer Bank, San Francisco, who was a pil-
lar of the church, and stole $2,000,000 from the depositors, and who denounced
the honest prayer of "Rattlin' Joe" as sacrilegious.

Ar' they bound to take lodgin's with Satan,
   While Duncan, the deacon, steals all?
An' pays with the sweat of the poor man
   The price for a sanctified stall?

Ar' they to be damn'd inter torment,
   An' driv through unquenchable flames,
'Cause the big book in front o' the pulpit
   Don't happen ter show up thar names?
Is the devil a-goin' for to yank 'em
   To his kingdom of fire down below,
Jist 'cause they don't jine in yer meetin's,
   And work in the very same row?

In short, can't a man as lives honest,
   An' don't take the devil inside
(For no man kin be a good Christian
   An' yet from his sideboard imbibe).
If he does every day to his neighbor
   As he'd have thet same neighbor to do,
Won't he fare jist as well at the clean-up
   As if worth a million or two?

The churches are good institutions;
   I like to hear good preachers tell
'Bout Christ and the good o' religion,
   But they ought ter preach temp'rance as well:
'Cause rum's the stronghold o' the devil,
   An' a man as drinks don't always win,
'Cause he never kin keep himself level,
   Since rum is a cuss and a sin.

But I tell ye, a man as lives honest,
   If he never hears tell o' the church,
Kin jist be as happy hereafter,
   And roost on the heavenly perch;
We're all in the way o' temptation,
   Thar's no one who's free from all sin;
But Christ won't go back on us poor folks
   If we do jist the best that we kin.

THE SCOUT'S REQUEST BEFORE THE BATTLE.

'Twas a moonlit night, just a year ago,
   As we sat and lay by the old camp fire.
"Come fill up yer pipes," said Muggins the scout,
   "And draw yoursel's up just a little nigher,

"An' I'll tell ye a story (the gospel truth),
   An' I reckon I couldn't lie to-night ;
For somehow I feel as if this poor chap
   Wer' goin' ter git left in to-morror's fight.

"An', pards, if I do—I see ye smile,
   But I ar' in earnest, you bet yer life,
Nor I arn't afeard to pass in my checks ;
   But, pards, I'm a-thinkin' of home and wife.

"I left the old cabin—now two weeks ago ;
   My poor wife's face wor a picter of sorror.
'Muggins,' said she, 'if ye get killed,
   Then God '—but, no matter, I go to-morror.

"Ye know me, boys ; now look ye here,
   Don't tell me I mustn't go in with you !
I never did weaken in all my life,
   An' to morror I'll lead them boys in blue.

"An' if, when the evenin' sun goes down,
   This time to-morror ye find I'm dead,
I want ye to tell me now, right here,
   Ye won't see my little ones want for bread.

"No ! thank the Lord ! but how about Jim ?
   Now, there ar' a boy as is like his dad,
An' 'Bat,' if ye say that you'll tend ter him,
   Why dyin' to-morror won't be so bad."

     *   *   *   *   *   *

Next eve, as the sun was going down,
   And firing had ceased along the line,
Old Muggins was humming that little song
   Of "Home, Sweet Home," in the bright sunshine,

When zip came a bullet, and Muggins fell.
 " Battees," he said, " Bat, don't forget
My wife—my Annie—my blue-eyed Mag,
    An' Jimmie—our Jimmie—his father's pet."

We covered him up with the mossy sod ;
    Renewed our promise above his grave ;
Left him alone—alone with his GoD—
    Muggins the scout, and Muggins the brave.

THE DEATH OF CUSTER.

In July, 1876, I received a telegram from W. F. Cody (Buffalo Bill), which read : " Have you heard of the death of our brave Custer?" I immediately wrote the following verses, which I sent Mr. Cody, in answer to his dispatch on the following day :

Did I hear the news from Custer?
　Well, I reckon I did, old pard ;
It came like a streak of lightin',
　And, you bet, it hit me hard.
I ain't no hand to blubber,
　And the briny ain't run for years ;
But chalk me down for a lubber,
　If I didn't shed regular tears.

What for ? Now look ye here, Bill,
　You're a bully boy, that's true ;
As good as e'er wore buckskin,
　Or fought with the boys in blue ;
But I'll bet my bottom dollar
　Ye had no trouble to muster
A tear, or perhaps a hundred,
　When ye heard of the death of Custer.

He always thought well of you, pard,
　And had it been Heaven's will,
In a few more days you'd met him,
　And he'd welcomed his old scout, Bill.
For, if ye remember, at Hat Creek
　I met ye with General Carr ;
We talked of the brave young Custer,
　And recounted his deeds of war.

But little we knew even then, pard
　(And that's just two weeks ago,
How little we dreamed of disaster,
　Or that he had met the foe)—

That the fearless, reckless hero,
　　So loved by the whole frontier,
Had died on the field of battle
　　In this our centennial year.

I served with him in the army,
　　In the darkest days of the war ;
And I reckon ye know his record,
　　For he was our guiding star.
And the boys who gathered round him
　　To charge in the early morn,
War just like the brave who perished
　　With him on the Little Horn.

And where is the satisfaction,
　　And how are we going to get square ?
By giving the Reds more rifles ?
　　Invite them to take more hair ?
We want no scouts, no trappers,
　　Nor men who know the frontier ?
Phil, old boy, you're mistaken —
　　You must have the volunteer.

They talk about peace with these demons
　　By feeding and clothing them well ;
I'd as soon think an angel from heaven
　　Would reign with contentment in hell ;
And some day these Quakers will answer
　　Before the great Judge of us all,
For the death of our daring young Custer,
　　And the boys who around him did fall.

Perhaps I am judging them harshly,
　　But I mean what I'm telling ye, pard ;
I'm letting them down mighty easy —
　　Perhaps they may think it is hard.
But I tell ye the day is approaching —
　　The boys are beginning to muster,
That day of the great retribution — .
　　The day of revenge for our Custer.

And I will be with you, friend Cody,
    My mite will go in with the boys ;
I shared all their hardships last winter,
    I shared all their sorrows and joys ;
So tell them I'm coming, friend William,
    I trust I will meet you ere long ;
Regards to the boys in the mountains,
    Yours truly, in friendship still strong.

COMRADE, WHY THIS LOOK OF SADNESS?

Written some years ago to the late Charley Reynolds, Custer's bravest and
best scout, who perished by his side on the Little Big Horn.

COMRADE, why this look of sadness?
    What has caused this sudden change?
Why thus wander in the moonlight,
    Acting so uncommon strange?
Know that I would share thy sorrow,
    Even shed a tear with thee ;
Sick or wounded would I leave you?
    No ! nor would you part from me.

Tell me, then ; I too, have sorrow,
    But I drive it from my mind ;
'Tis but folly thus to borrow
    Trouble from the midnight wind.
Come, there's music at the barracks,
    We're having quite a hop to-night—
Have a dance with little Jessie,
    And I'm sure you'll feel all right.

No? Ah, comrade, I can see it,
    Even though you will not tell ;
You have loved with all your nature—
    Loved not wisely, but too well.

This it is that makes you gloomy—
   Cuts you to the very core ;
But you must remember, Charley,
   There are very many more.

So, at last, I've got your secret—
   Only one ?　Indeed ! not more?
Me ?　Why, man, that ain't a marker—
   I can count them by the score.
Women—why, of course, they're fickle,
   But the men are fickle, too,
And I'm sure the greater number
   Of the fairer sex are true.

Yes, I had *one* little sweetheart ;
   Do you see that blackened spot ?
There it was that I first met her
   In her father's little cot ;
And beside this mossy willow,
   When the skylark's music fell,
Gertie told me how she loved me,
   'Mid the fragrance of the dell.

While my arms were fondly twining
   Round her little form so fair,
Bright blue eyes like diamonds shining,
   And the moonbeams kissed her hair—
Then it was a silent arrow
   Pierced my little girl and I—
Pierced her through the heart, God help me—
   Me to live and she to die.

Here, beside this dear old willow,
   Where the flowers are growing wild,
Rests old Bruce, the guide and trapper,
   With my love, his only child.
Rest in peace, my little darling,
   There is joy in Heaven for you ;
As for me—*no peace, no resting*
   While there lives a single Sioux.

Now, my boy, you know the reason
　　Why I seek this spot alone ;
When the moon is up and shining,
　　I can watch beside my own.
Go, enjoy yourself—I cannot,
　　While my angel sleeps close by.
Hark ! get down—I see a scalp-lock !
　　Not a word—he, too, must die.

Death was silent in his mission—
　　Not the faintest sound was heard ;
While the scout, with cat-like motion,
　　Moved as if he were a bird ;
Then the flash of steel by moonlight—
　　Not a word had yet been said ;
But the brave young lover conquered—
　　Scored another for the dead.

BY THE LAKE.

My heart is just dancing with rapture
　　To the music that springs from the soul,
As I revel in Nature's seclusion,
　　Where God left His name on her scroll.
And the birds seem to ask for a token—
　　For a something that they may retain—
A song that the soul may have spoken,
　　By the streamlet that flows to the plain.

And here far away in the wildwood,
　　With Nature, unsullied by art,
Those thoughts that were dear to my childhood
　　Still twine themselves close round my heart.
Sing on, sweetest songsters, thy singing
　　Bright memory's slumbers awake ;
Thy voices in sweet chorus ringing—
　　So I leave you in peace by the lake.

"GOD BLESS YE, GENER'L CUSTER."

" By gosh, I ar' as hungry
　　As a prairie wolf, you bet,
An', pards, I won't forget ye,
　　An' am moughty glad we met.
Yer see, I've been ter prospec',
　　An' I lost my latitud'.
Laws'ee, but I war hungry,
　　Them beans war moughty good.

" I've see'd thet face afore, pards—
　　Can't say as how I know,
My eyes ain't wot they us' ter war
　　'Bout fifteen year ago.
But, dog my cats, I'll swar it,
　　Let's take a closer sight—
Blest if it arn't the Gener'l !
　　I knew I must be right."

And then a pearly tear drop
　　Stood in the old man's eye.
" Yer know I've pray'd ter see him
　　Jist once afore I'd die ;
He saved my wife and baby
　　When the reds began to muster."
With outstretched hand he, sobbing, said :
　　" God bless ye, Gener'l Custer !"

" I reckin ye don't remember
　　Old Bill as run the mail
From Sidney up to Red Cloud,
　　When ye war on the trail;
An' how thet frosty mornin'
　　Yer saved my Tommy's life,
An' took a heap o' chances—
　　She told me—Jane, my wife.

" I warn't thar to thank yer
   When I heerd the story through,
'Cause that war all I had ter give,
   An' all as I could do ;
An', Gener'l, if yer wants me,
   "Tain't much as I kin do,
But, dog my cats, I'm ready
   To trump death's ace for you."

"NEVER GIVE UP THE SHIP!"

In the spring of 1875, in Custer City, at the time I wrote the following verses, I was, to say the least, sick and tired of the mountains. I had just nursed to life old Charley S——, from Chicago, an old Forty-niner (who was always kind to me), while a man named Hughes lay on one of my bunks, his arm shattered by a bullet from the wrist to the muscle, and Jule Seminole, one of my scouts, a faithful Cheyenne warrior, lay on the other bunk, with pneumonia. I had hard work to watch Jule. If I ever left the cabin during the day, and the sun was shining, he would be sure to jump out of bed, run around the cabin with only a single blanket thrown around him, and squat right down on a log or stone, his moccasined feet in the melting snow; and when I tried to reason with him, and scold him for exposing himself, he would look at me with his great brown eyes, shake his head and say : "You heap good to me; me know you like I get well. But me no like white man's medicine. Too much bad taste. Sun heap better big medicine." He always returned to his bunk, however, and finally got well again, and proved his devotion to me afterward on many occasions, never losing sight of me while on the trail. Hughes had a little boy nine years old, who relieved me occasionally, and watched while I slept. I never took my clothes off, night or day, except to change my underwear, for I only had a buffalo robe and one blanket, which I spread on the damp sawdust floor; and only for a strong constitution and temperate habits, I, too, would have been laid up. One evening, a merchant, who had just come in the Hills, called to see me, and when I told him how I was situated, how I had to hunt for my meat, and how discouraged I was beginning to feel, he remarked : "Never get down-hearted, Jack— *never give up the ship !*" And, although he was well off in this world's goods, he never offered me a pound of tea or a piece of bacon. After he left my cabin, while my single tallow candle cast a sickly light upon the smoked logs, I wrote, "Never Give up the Ship !"

"NEVER give up the ship, old boy!"
  Said a friend to me to-night;
"But jog along with a manly step,
  And with spirits always light;
Laugh with a hearty will, old boy,
  And wait for the turn of the tide,
For this is a beautiful world of ours—
  So, Jack, let your troubles slide."

How easy it is for *him* to say
  "Never give up the ship!"
While thinking of a gas-lit home,
  And I with a tallow dip,
Ensconsed in my little log caboose,
  The wolf and the snow at the door;
I wish I could give up the craft,
  I'd sail in her no more.

"Never give up the ship!" he said,
  This *friend!* I could almost curse;
With love and friends and a happy home—
  Ah! yes, and a bottomless purse.
How easy it is for one to say,
  "'There's better luck in store,"
When hunger and sickness pass him by
  And knock at another's door.

When home for him is a safe retreat,
  And nothing to worry or fret,
While I in the snow must hunt my meat—
  Or what? Why, starve, you bet.
Two comrades wounded, sick and sore,
  Are stretched on the bunks beside,
While I shake down on the sawdust floor
  And wake with a sore-marked hide.

Old Charley too has just got well!
  He told me I saved his life,
And how I loved to hear him tell
  Of his home and his dear good wife,

And how, if ever I went back East,
  His folks I must call and see.
Then, old boy, we will have a feast,
  And drink your good health in tea.

Well, I don't intend to give up the ship,
  But I wish I could find a canoe,
And we were two hundred miles from here,
  On the banks of the old Mossu—
I reckon we'd float, would Jule and I,
  Though we worked our venison raw,
And never let up till we gazed once more
  On the spires of Omaha.

MUSING.

(*To the Man of Intellect.*)

These verses were written in answer to an anonymous letter written by some one in Victoria, B. C. (who was English, you know), telling me to desist from imposing my doggerel on an intelligent newspaper public.

WHILE with various thoughts and feelings
  I am musing here to-night—
Thoughts of other years of sorrow,
  Feelings of a heart more light—
Musing still, and still I wonder
  What my future lot will be,
While my soul is craving knowledge,
  Will not fortune smile on me?

Is there *no* poetic beauty
  In those simple songs of mine?
Must a man be bred in college
  Ere he dares to form a rhyme?
Though his soul dictates the music,
  Yet his words, uncouth and plain,

Must not find a friendly welcome
   From the learned man of brain.

While my beating heart oft whispers
   Sweetest music to my soul,
And I feel that heaven-born passion
   Which I care not to control,
That which 'neath the spreading branches
   Often caused my mates to start,
Aye! and list with awe and wonder
   To the songs which left my heart.

Far away in wild Dakota,
   Hours I've stood upon the green,
Spouting what I thought poetic,
   Only by my comrades seen,
Revelling in nature's grandeur.
   Ah! but those were happy days,
For I thought I *was* a poet,
   And deserving of some praise.

Yet, alas! here comes a letter
   Telling me I must desist,
Written by—perhaps George Francis—
   Such a s-*Train* was to his fist.
Stop it, Jack—let reason guide you,
   Good advice you dare reject,
And you'll get another letter
   From a man of *intellect*.

Every man is not a classic,
   Nearly all who labor read—
These at least peruse my verses,
   Sometimes even with a greed.
Let me, then, a little longer
   Pass like this my idle hours;
Time will surely make me stronger—
   Spring must come to bring the flowers.

IN THE MOUNTAINS, CARIBOO, B. C.

AN EPITAPH ON WILD BILL.

The following epitaph on J. B. Hickock (Wild Bill) was written while sitting on his grave, near Deadwood, on the 10th of September, 1876.

SLEEP on, brave heart, in peaceful slumber,
   Bravest scout in all the West ;
Lightning eyes and voice of thunder,
   Closed and hushed in quiet rest.
     Peace and rest at last is given ;
     May we meet again in heaven.
       Rest in peace.

GRIZZLY JAKE.

WE sat by the smoking camp-fire,
    On the eve of a summer's day ;
There was Grizzly Jake, and Yankee Jim,
    And whole-soul'd Pete McKay ;
There was little Bessie and Annie Roe,
    And Flora, the pet of the train ;
There were noble women and hardy men,
    Who had started across the plain.

Old Grizzly Jake was our leader,
    And the bravest in all the train ;
His home was among the mountains,
    His camp was the rolling plain ;
But his heart bore a heavy burden,
    And his face wore wrinkles of care,
But his eyes were as bright as the eagle's,
    Though frosted his once golden hair.

He sat by my side this evening,
    On the trunk of a fallen tree,
When Flora, our blue-eyed darling,
    Came over and sat on his knee.
"Untle Jake," said the child, "I do love 'oo ;
    And mamma said 'oo feel so bad,
Taus 'oo hasn't no 'ittle F'ora—
    Is 'at why 'oo always feel sad?"

Great drops stood in beads on his forehead,
    And tears rolled away from his eyes,
As he answered : "My Jean and my Flora
    Are waiting for me in the skies.
Yes, darling, I had a sweet Flora,
    And Jean was her mother—my wife.
Aye, dead ! Oh, God ! it was fearful !
    Cut down in the morning of life.

"And still—but why should I think it—
  My Flora may still be alive ;
Yet I saw in her breast the cold arrow.
  No, no ; she could never survive.
No, child, it is too long a story,
  And perhaps it would cause you a fright.
There, now, run away to your mamma."
  "Untle Jake, let me tiss 'oo dood-night."

"Good-night, and God bless you, my angel!
  Oh, God !" said the old pioneer,
"Thou only can know my deep sorrow ;
  And, God ! Thou art all whom I fear.
Nor hell, with its fury, can daunt me,
  And, death, I would welcome thee still ;
But the fiends have not all departed,
  And one there is left, I *must kill.*"

The camp was as still as the night wind—
  Not a sound, save the stirring of leaves—
As the scout strolled off to the river,
  And walked to and fro 'neath the trees,
Until long after midnight, still walking,
  He saw (yet he seemed not to see)
The head of a Sioux in the willows.
  "It was Flora who sent me," said he.

He knew what was coming at daybreak,
  Nor feared, while yet dark, for his life ;
For he knew they'd not dare to attack him,
  Except with the arrow or knife ;
So he kept out of range of such weapons,
  And carelessly walked to the train,
Where he lay down, and spoke in a whisper,
  Lest fright and confusion might reign.

And soon every man in the outfit
  Was piling up bacon and flour,
Inside of the wheels of each wagon.
  The morning would dawn in an hour.

The relief for the three-o'clock herder
  Went out with his orders O. K.
Said Jake: "Round your cattle up slowly ;
  We'll corral them at break of day."

Every woman and child was still sleeping,
  And all were prepared for the fight,
When our pet of the train, little Flora,
  Awoke from a dream, in a fright ;
And, seeing old Jake with his rifle,
  She whispered these words in his ear :
"Untle Jake, while asleep, I was d'eaming
  Dat 'oo 'ittle F"ora was here."

"God bless you !" again said Old Grizzly,
  And he whispered these words in her ear :
"Keep low till I come again, darling ;
  I believe that my angels are here."
"Twenty men," said the old man of sixty,
  "Fleet-footed, with nerves that are steel,
Follow me, while the morning is darkest.
  Good angels are with us, I feel.

"And you who remain with your sweethearts,
  And you who must fight for your wives,
Be guided by me, I entreat you,
  And we will not lose precious lives ;
And, men, when you bring up your rifles—
  Don't mind though these devils may yell ;
It is only a ruse to stampede you—
  Just look through your sights, and look well.

"Don't fire till within twenty paces—
  By that time each face you can see.
They believe all are sleeping ; and, comrades,
  Just aim 'twixt the shoulder and knee,
While we strike for their rear in the sage-brush.
  No fear—by the time we are seen,
You will have struck for the living,
  And I for my Flora and Jean."

Uncle Jake and his twenty departed.
  Not a man, not a woman or child
But believed in his grit and his goodness ;
  And the pet of the train sweetly smiled,
As she whispered, "He's dust 'ike the Sav'or ;
  And, mamma, 1 ain't dot no fear,
Taus Dod sent his F'ora his angel
  To tell him bad Ingins were here.

*   *   *   *   *   *

On the field there are fifty GOOD Indians,
  And all looking peaceful and bland.
Perhaps they have gone to be angels,
  Perhaps they have gone to be d——d;
And perhaps Grizzly Jake will recover,
  And look on his angel and queen,
For Flora is smoothing his ringlets,
  And bathing his temple—his Jean.

BIRDS OF THE HUDSON BAY.

  EVERY day when I open the door
  Of my little cabin, I see before
  Two little birds—a happy pair,
  Sitting, and cooing, and twittering there—
  Sitting and waiting, perched on a bough,
  And never afraid of me—somehow
  Waiting to see the door open wide :
  Then in a moment, close to my side,
  They come and chirrup, but never sing—
  Chirrup for crumbs, waiting for spring—
  Spring that will come, melting the snow,
  Then my pets will leave me* and go
  Off to the meadows, happy and gay,
  Beautiful birds of the Hudson Bay.

* Hudson Bay birds (natives of British Columbia).

MY IDEAS.

While in Barkerville, B. C., a certain California expert condemned the quartz, and said we had no ledges; in answer to which I wrote the following verses:

BARKER, I love thy rustic hills,
　　I love thy streams and bowers;
I've lingered near thy rippling rills,
　　And gathered sweetest flowers;　　·
And down thy wondrous valleys,
　　And up each snow-clad peak,
I've wandered where the roses
　　Of nature's grandeur speak.

Oh, where in God's creation,
　　Can we poor people go,
And find a better prospect
　　Than these our croppings show?
And tell me, oh, ye experts,
　　From whence the millions came,
That rolled out in the sluices,
　　Since Barker got its name?

And if there are no ledges
　　In this little world of ours,
Go cast aside your sledges,
　　And pluck your budding flowers.
Go draw your stakes and burn them,
　　And cache your mining tools,
And tell the whole creation
　　That you're a set of fools.

And then, when you have vanished,
　　Some kid-gloved millionaire
Will step into your country,
　　And call it wondrous fair.
And ere your hair is silvered,
　　The news will come to you:
" The world has nothing richer
　　Than the mines of Cariboo."

THE PROSPECTOR'S SOLILOQUY.

While sitting one day at one of our mining claims in the Black Range of New Mexico, discussing the propriety of sinking a shaft, my pard, Jim Blain, better known as "Apache Jim," arose, and, striking a tragic attitude, cried out: "To sink, or not to sink? that's the question." This incident suggested the following:

To sink or not to sink?　That is the question ;
Whether 'tis fitter in the prospector to sell
The highly metalliferous croppings for a song,
Or, using muscle, to dig down,
And thus, by perseverance, strike it rich.
To work, to sink, and by that sinking strike a lead
Of gold or silver, or finest copper glance
That luck is heir to.　'Tis a consummation
Devoutly to be wished.　To sink, to blast ;
To blast, perchance to bu'st—aye ! there's the rub,
For at a shallow depth what base may come
When we have shovelled off th' uncertain top
Must give us pause.　There's the respect
Which makes calamity of a prospect-hole ;
For who can tell what pinch may come below
The argentiferous stuff—component parts of lead,
The metalliferous decomposed conglomerate
Eruption of nature, all broken up ; perchance
The insolence of luckier pards, and then
The chance the miner takes by sinking shaft,
While he himself might be much better off
By simply waiting.　What is 't we would not do
But that the dread of something yet unseen,
The undiscovered pay-streak (perhaps not there),
That makes us rather raise the monuments we have
Than open up the ground we know not of.
Thus prospecting makes cowards of us all,
And so the prospects of a big bonanza
Are sicklied o'er by some dark, cussed doubt,
And speculators in a surface prize
Do thus regard their interest, turn aside,
And lose, perchance, a million !

THE MINER'S DREAM — XMAS EVE.

To my Comrade and Brother, T. W. Keene.

It was Christmas eve, and the pale moon smiled
    Through the silvery clouds of gray ;
The scene was grand—in nature wild—
    And stars shone bright as day ;
And, all alone by his stony hearth,
    A miner, young and strong,
Thinking of all he loved on earth,
    Sat, singing this little song :

SONG AND CHORUS.

Dedicated to every one who has Loved Ones far away.

Dearest Annie, I am thinking,
    While the night winds whisper low,
Of my loving wife and babies,
    And my heart is all aglow ;
For I've struck it in the gravel,
    And our home will soon be free ;
So I write to tell you, darling,
    Kiss the little ones for me.

Chorus.

Kiss the little ones for papa ;
    Tell them, in their joy and glee,
How I love our little darlings—
    Kiss the little ones for me.

Tell our darlings it is twilight,
    While the shades of evening fall,
And I'm gazing on their shadows,
    On their baby faces small ;
How I dwell upon each feature,
    Full of love and ecstasy,
While I kiss our babies' pictures—
    Kiss the little ones for me.
                                    Chorus.

Tell the little ones I'm coming,
  When they go to bed each night,
As they whisper, "God bless papa!"
  With their baby faces bright.
I have *written to the banker*—
  You have waited patiently;
While I dream of home, my Annie,
  Kiss the little ones for me.

                    Chorus.

*   *   *   *   *   *

The tears rolled down his swarthy cheek,
  And the heart that knew no fear
Beat faster as he heard her speak—
  Or, rather, seemed to hear
His Annie's voice, so low and sweet,
  In answer to his lay:
"Dear Harry, we again shall meet,
  While love is in its May."

"Oh, happy dream! If dream it be—
  I'll lay me here till dawn,
And close my eyes, that I may see
  This happy scene go on."
And while the glowing embers died
  Upon the stony hearth,
He wandered back to Annie's side,
  The spot most dear on earth.

He dreamed that all was gloomy there
  At twilight Christmas eve—
The children cold, the larder bare,
  And no one to relieve.
And, listening through a broken glass,
  He heard his dear wife say:
"Don't cry, my darlings—yet, alas!
  To-morrow's Christmas day!"

Oh, how his manly bosom heaved—
  His face was all aglow;

"My darlings soon shall be relieved.
  I'll go right in—but, no !
Old Santa Claus shall play his part ;
  I'll dress him to his eyes,
And fill each little saddened heart
  With joy and sweet surprise."

And as the rays of morning light
  Were peeping o'er the hill,
Old Santa Claus, with hair snow-white,
  Sat down on the window-sill,
Weary and loaded with precious freight
  From his back to the cutter-sled.
"Ha, ha !" he laughed, "I'm not too late—
  They're just getting out of bed."

The children's tongues were loose again,
  And their eyes were opened wide ;
The rags were gone from the broken pane,
  And three stockings hung inside.
The largest stocking was long and red,
  And lettered with gold and bright ;
"This is for little Jack," it said,
  While little May's was white ;

And the third for Annie, the faithful wife.
  "Oh, mamma, mamma dear !"
Said Jack, while showing a pearly knife,
  "Old Santa Claus was here !"
"And, mamma," said little May, whose eyes
  Were beaming with delight,
"Dod heard our prayers up in a sties,
  'Tos we prayed so hard las' night.

"Yes, darlings, God has heard your prayers,
  And smiled behind the frown."
Old Santa Claus had climbed up-stairs,
  And now came tumbling down ;
And such a sight was never seen
  By mortal eyes before,

While Santa Claus, the miner king,
  With good things strewed the floor.

Then quick he threw aside his staff,
  The white beard from his face,
While 'mid a storm of cry and laugh,
  And three in one embrace,
The happy miner said that day
  He never more would roam ;
And thus, two thousand miles away,
  He spent his Christmas home.

   *   *   *   *   *

"Consarn my picter! Harry, lad ;
  Laws-ee ! yer ain't up yet?
Why, boy, what makes yer look so sad?
  Thar's somethin' wrong, I'll bet ;
Corral me if yer don't look sick !
  Wa'al, pshaw ! I'll jest prescribe—
Thar's hur letter, long and thick—
  That's why I tuck this ride.

"I'll bet two beaver-skins agin
  A starved coyotte's pelt,
And all the ore on Jennie Lynn
  That's worth a darn to smelt,
As that's a daisy Christmas-box
  To drive away the blues.
So, Harry lad, let this old fox
  Go off and take a snooze."

Hold on, old pard ! this is, indeed,
  A Christmas-box for me—
The medicine I sorely need—
  I'll share it, pard, with thee.
From Annie, 'way back in the East ;
  My fears were all absurd.
To-day they'll have a glorious feast—
  The *banker's* kept his word.

FORT CRAIG, NEW MEXICO.

"OUR NUGGET."

MAY CODY CRAWFORD.

Some call her blue eyes,
  And some call her pet,
Violet and sunshine,
  And sweet mignonette ;
Golden hair, blue bird,
  And sweet little love,
But I call her May flower,
  My little white dove.

Chorus.

May flower, May flower,
  Budding in beauty and love,
Daffodil dimples and daisies,
  I call her my little white dove.

Eyes like her mother's,
  And lips like a peach ;
Cheeks like two apples
  That's just out of reach ;
Ears like bright amber,
  With gold hair above,
My own little May flower,
  My little white dove.

Chorus.

God bless our darling
  And keep her alway,
Guide her through flow'rets
  On each coming May.
Teach her to love us,
  As much as we love
Rosy cheeks, blue eyes,
  Our little white dove.

Chorus.

BUFFALO CHIPS, THE SCOUT.

To Buffalo Bill.

The following verses on the life and death of poor old Buffalo Chips are founded entirely on facts. His death occurred on September 8th, 1876, at Slim Buttes. He was within three feet of me when he fell, uttering the words credited to him below.

THE evenin' sun war settin', droppin' slowly in the west,
An' the soldiers, tired an' tuckered, in the camp would find that rest
Which the settin' sun would bring 'em, for they marched since break o'
    day—
Not a bite to eat 'cept horses as war killed upon the way ;
For, ye see, our beans an' crackers, an' our pork war outen sight,
An' the boys expected rashuns when they struck our camp that night ;
For a little band had started for to bring some cattle on,
An' they struck an Indian village, which they captured jist at dawn.

Wall, I war with that party when we captured them ar' Sioux,
An' we quickly sent a courier to tell old Crook the news.
Old Crook ! I should say Gener'l, cos he war with the boys—
Shared his only hard-tack, our sorrows and our joys ;
An' thar is one thing sartin—he never put on style.
He'd greet the scout or soldier with a social kinder smile,
An' that's the kind o' soldier as the prairy likes to get,
An' every man would trump death's ace for Crook or Miles, you bet.

But I'm kinder off the racket, cos these Gener'ls gets enough
O' praise 'ithout my chippin', so I'll let up on that puff ;
For I want ter tell a story 'bout a mate of mine as fell,
Cos I loved the honest fellar, an' he did his dooty well ;
Buffalo Chips we call'd him, but his other name war White ;
I'll tell yo how he got that name, an' reckon I am right.
You see, a lot of big-bugs an' officers came out
One time to hunt th' buffaler, an' fish for speckled trout.

Wall, little Phil—ye've heerd on him, a dainty little cuss
As rode his charger twenty miles to stop a little muss.
Well, Phil, he said ter Jonathin, whose other name war White ;
" You go an' find them buffaler, an' see you get 'em right."

So White he went an' found 'em, an' he found 'em sech a band
As he sed would set 'em crazy, an' little Phil looked bland ;
But when the outfit halted, one bull was all war there,
Then Phil he call him "Buffalo Chips," an' swore a little sware.

Wall, White he kinder liked it, cos the Gener'l called him Chips,
An' he us'ter wear two shooters in a belt above his hips.
Then he said :" Now, look ye, Gener'l, since ye've called me that ar' name,
Jist around them little sand-hills is yer dog-gone pesky game."
But when the hunt war over, an' the table spread for lunch,
The Gener'l called for glasses, an' wanted his in punch ;
An' when the punch was punished, the Gener'l smacked his lips,
While squar' upon the table sot a dish o' *Buffalo Chips.*

The Gener'l looked confounded, an' he also looked for White,
But Jonathin he reckon'd it war better he should lite ;
So he skinned across the prairy, cos, ye see, he didn't mind
A *chippin'* any longer while the Gener'l saw the *blind,*
Fur the Gener'l would *a-raised him,* if he'd jist held up his hand,
But he thought he wouldn't *see him,* cos he didn't hev the sand,
An' he rode as fast—aye, faster, than the Gener'l did that day,
Like lightin' down from Winchester, some twenty miles away.

Wall, White he had no cabin, an' no home ter call his own,
So Buffaler Bill he took him an' shared with him his home.
An' how he loved Bill Cody ! By gosh ! it war a sight
Ter see him watch his shadder an' foller him at night,
Cos Bill war kinder hated by a cussed gang o' thieves
As carried pistols in thar belts an' bowies in thar sleeves ;
An' Chips he never left him for fear he'd get a pill,
Nor would he think it moughty hard to die for Buffalo Bill.

We us'ter mess together—that ar' Chips an' Bill an' me ;
An' ye oughter watch his movements ; it would do ye good ter see
How he us'ter cook them wittles, an' gather lots o' greens
To mix up with the juicy pork, an' them unruly beans.
An' one cold, chilly mornin' he bought a lot o' corn,
An' a little flask o' likker, as cost fifty cents a horn.
Tho' *forty yards* war nowhar, it war finished soon, ye bet ;
But, friends, I *promised some one,* and I'm strong teetotal yet.

It war twenty-fourth o' August, in the last Centennial year,
We bid farewell to Cody an' gave a hearty cheer ;
An' Chips said, lookin' after : " I may never see him more,
Nor meet him in his cabin as I us'ter do of yore,
Whar I us'ter take his babies an' buy each one a toy,
An' play with them ar' younkers jist like a great big boy."
An' when the cold lead struck him—" Jack, boy," said he, " you tell—'
He stopped, then said : "Bless Cody, the babies—all—farewell."

He's sleepin' in the mountains, near a little runnin' brook,
Thar's not a soul to see him, 'cept the angels take a look,
Or a butterfly may linger on his grave at early morn—
No mortal eye may see it till old Gabriel toots his horn ;
For we laid him 'neath the foot trail that the Sioux might never know,
As they'd dig him up and scalp him if they had the slightest show ;
An' we marched two thousand footmen and horsemen o'er his breast—
Without a stone to mark the spot, we left the scout to rest.

An' then I sent a telegraph and tol' Bill he war dead ;
I'll give in full his answer, an' this war what he said :
" Poor White, he war my truest friend.   My wife and children, too,
Have wept as if he war our own.   An', Jack, I ask of you
To write a little verse for us in mem'ry o' poor White."
So that war Cody's telegraph, an' that is why I write ;
But laws'ee ! my book-larnin' ar' shaky for a bard—
I can't jist do him justice, but Heaven holds *his* reward.

TO JAMES G. FAIR.

MY FRIEND.

DEAR friend, I have a word to say to you,
Something to tell ; perhaps you never knew
Half my distress, the shock of Fortune's frown,
That bore me down to earth, and kept me down,
Till you, with generous heart, made clear the way ;
Gave hope where hope was dead—a sunny ray

Dispersed the clouds that overhung my sky,
And made my crutches to the four winds fly.
Oh, sir, had I a heart of stone,
Instead of flesh and blood, I'd gladly own
That you have made of me this very day
A man, but in a different way
From kicks and frowns (by which some men are made),
By starting me a little up the grade.
" *Now help yourself !*" I thank you from my heart
For those last words, because they form a part
Of this new life—and make my bosom thrill—
A beacon light to guide me up life's hill.
Once there, upon the summit of its brow,
My heart will speak as it is speaking now ;
From out its greatest depths will breathe a name
That made me in my joy forget that I was lame.
Then—Heaven helping every act of mine
Will prove my gratefulness for one of thine.
So let me live that you may proudly say,
I was his *friend in need*, and am to-day.

San Francisco, September, 1879.

CUSTER.

To General Wesley Merritt, Custer's Friend and Comrade.

"No spot on the American Continent," says Major Newsom, in his "Black Hills Sketches," is "so grand and beautiful as Custer. Lying peacefully in a basin, French Creek winding through it, and the ground gently ascending even to the apex of Harney's Peak, the scene is lovely beyond description. In front of the city a high mountain rears its head ; just outside of the line of houses a bluff surrounds the place in a semicircle, and from this bluff no grander view ever fell upon the vision of man. Talk about scenery in Europe! It is tame in comparison with that about Custer. Gazing out from this point no sight could be more enchanting. Here at our feet is the city, so clean and regular. Yonder is an undulating plain, as charming as the graceful figure of a woman ; on our left winds the road ; on our right, swelling knolls, hillocks, valleys, and just beyond, grand, natural avenues, three hundred feet wide, on either side of which are uplifts of rocks, and on the top of which are trees. Further on are parks, grottos, rills, vales, streams, valleys, mountains, and every element necessary to make a most imposing scene. These avenues are lined with trees, and the small road which winds through them reminds one of the magnificent domain of an English lord rather than nature's handiwork. An artificial park of this character would cost at least ten million dollars.

There's a spot in the woodland
  My heart longs to see,
Where streamlets are dancing
  With laughter and glee ;
Where the sweet daffodil
  And the daisies are seen,
And the deer loves to sport
  On its mantle of green.

Chorus.

In the valley of Custer,
The park with its cluster
Of little log cabins spread out on the green.
'Tis the valley of Custer,
Where oft we did muster,
And drank to the brave from the soldier's canteen.

Oh, the flower of that valley,
  Whose bright name it bears,
Now sleeps near the river,
  Away from life's cares.
But still there's a spot
  Holds his mem'ry most dear,
The heart of each comrade—
  Each brave pioneer.
                              Chorus.

The pine trees are sighing
  On hill-tops around ;
We hear not his voice,
  Nor the sweet bugle sound.
Our tears wet the sod
  On that terrible morn,
When God *called the roll*
  On the " Little Big Horn."
                              Chorus.

GOOD-BY.

To one who had been very kind to me, and watched by my bedside night and day until convalescent, after a severe wound.

Good-by, my darling, since you must away
    To other scenes, and other hearts to greet you ;
With me I could not longer ask you stay,
    Besides, my dear, I know not how to treat you.
You and I have led a different life—
    You among the best and most refined,
While I afloat upon a sea of strife
    With vulgar men—the roughest of mankind.

And yet, this heart that beats alone for thee—
    This heart that learned to love blue eyes so well—
Is just as tender as a child's could be,
    And *you* can make it *heaven* for me—ah ! well.
Oh, darling, you can never know.   God knows
    The feelings of a heart so nearly broken.
And you, at times, as cold as mountain snows,
    With not one word of love—one little token.

If I, deep in my heart, could feel
    That you were mine—and mine alone—for life,
That you would, trusting to my strong arms, steal,
    And some day let me call you *little wife.*
Oh, God ! the thought most drives me mad, indeed !
    And why ?   Your actions merit not the thought,
For now you're almost anxious to be freed
    E'en from my sight—and will I be forgot ?

If so, then say the word.   Do say
    You do not love me, for suspense is pain ;
Tell me, darling, ere you go away,
    If I have loved my blue-eyed girl in vain ?
If so, 'tis better, dear, for you and me—
    Better if the truth to me you tell—
Better, though it breaks one heart, that we
    Should meet no more—but say a last farewell !

THE FIRST THAT DIED.

About eight o'clock one evening, in the winter of 1875, while I was washing the dishes after supper in my cabin, two travellers entered, hungry, weary, and footsore. After preparing supper, and giving them a warm corner by the glowing log fire, they told the following story: The elder man, John A. Byers, formerly captain of a company in a Maryland regiment, started from Sioux City for the Hills, and was joined next day by his companion, Charley, a boy about eighteen years of age. They had travelled five hundred miles, carrying their provisions and blankets, and after escaping a hundred dangers reached Custer City almost exhausted. They stayed at my cabin for nearly a week, when Byers went to Deadwood. Charley remained and went to work building himself a shelter. In company with another boy they dug a hole in the ground, about two feet and a half deep, and then carried poles on their shoulders with which they made a roof, making their dugout about three logs high all round. After covering the roof with boughs, they spaded about two feet of clay on the top. Two nights after the roof broke through, killing Charley outright, and nearly killing his companion. The saddest point about this affecting incident was that no letters, papers, or even the slightest clew to his home or friends could be found; all that we knew was that he had walked all the way from Sioux City to the Black Hills to die and start a graveyard. On that day, while sitting on the green beside his demolished cabin, I wrote these lines:

> Poor Charley braved the wintry storms,
>   And footed it all the way ;
> And now he is a bleeding corpse—
>   He died at dawn to-day.
> His is the old, old story—
>   He saw bright prospects here ;
> He left his home, his friends and all—
>   Perhaps a mother dear.
>
> If so, God pity that mother,
>   Perhaps alone and poor ;
> When some one breaks the blighting news
>   Her heart will break, I'm sure,
> To think she never, never more
>   Will clasp him to her breast ;
> Among the peaks in Custer Park
>   Poor Charley now must rest.

Comrades here in the golden land
  Will drop a silent tear
For those poor Charley left behind—
  A sister or mother dear.
Perhaps some blue-eyed little girl,
  With sunshine on her brow,
Is down upon her bended knees
  And praying for him now.

Down in the glade beside the brook
  Our boy shall sleep to-morrow ;
His weary march of life is o'er,
  Now free from care and sorrow.
And while we think of home, and love,
  And better days in store,
We humbly pray to Him above,
  And bow to Heaven once more.

THOSE EYES

Written in Cariboo, B. C., on looking at the photo of an old sweetheart.

WE meet as strangers now.   Those eyes—
  Those dreamy eyes—whose love-light shone
On me like sunbeams from the skies,
  And gazed so fondly in mine own,
No more have warmth, love, light, no more
For me, as in the days of yore.

Those witching eyes of heavenly blue,
  Beneath long silken lashes dreaming,
While far from her in Cariboo
  I oft have tried to solve their meaning ;
While something whispers as I sigh—
Old boy, those flames were all a lie.

THE PICNIC BY THE BROOK.

SONG AND DANCE.

Written for Miss Nellie McHenry, of Saulsbury's Troubadours.

I HAVE wandered o'er the prairie
    When the roses were in bloom ;
I have listened to the streamlets
    In the cheery month of June ;
While the mocking-birds were singing
    I have listened in the dell,
But nothing ever cheered me
    Like the voice of little Nell.

Chorus.

For she's sweeter than the lilies by the brook,
    And her voice is like the streamlets in the dell ;
It echoes back from every little nook,
    And the stars are not so bright as little Nell.

By the brook she sang so sweetly
    That my heart was all aglow,
And then she danced so neatly,
    With her light fantastic toe,
Can you wonder I was captured ?
    But I fear it's wrong to tell
How I enjoyed that picnic
    By the brook with little Nell.
                        Chorus.

She's as pretty as a picture,
    And her heart is full of glee,
And how my heart was beating
    When she looked and smiled on me.
But, indeed, I'll never whisper
    How in love with her I fell ;
For I hear she's got a lover,
    This bewitching little Nell.
                        Chorus.

Yet, no matter where I wander,
  Over prairie, land or sea,
The rippling of the waters
  Will repeat her songs to me.
Tho' she leaves for far Australia,
  I shall always wish her well—
Good-by to brookside picnics
  And the voice of little Nell.

Chorus.

AFTER TAPS.

Dear comrades, Grant is laid away,
  Our chief has gone to rest;
What matter where they plant his clay,
  To you who loved him best?
And since the North and South combine,
  'Twas all he asked from you,
Though after taps his deeds will shine
  Till Gabriel sounds tattoo.

And how your thoughts went back again
  To days of long ago,
When near him, at the battle's front,
  With loyal hearts aglow.
And as you marched behind his bier
  From morn till set of sun,
You thought he must be very near
  To Abe and Washington.

And Lee was there to greet him, too,
  And say, " Friend Grant, just see,
The sunny South has sent Fitz-Hugh
  To say a word for me."
There's Gordon too, and Little Phil;
  There's Sherman, Buck, and Joe,
And Stonewall says 'tis Heaven's will—
  There's peace and love below.

KIT CARSON.

(*Adios, Companero.*)

ADIOS, dear old hero, in peace may you slumber,
  Adown near the banks of the old Rio Grande ;
We think of thy daring with awe and with wonder,
  As near to thy tomb now uncovered we stand.

A rude, simple tablet, a plain slab of marble,
  Is all that your comrades have placed o'er your grave.
Sleep on, loyal heart, while the wild song-birds warble
  An anthem of praise to the deeds of the brave.

The veil of the future thy brave soul hath riven
  To drink in the sweetest celestial joys ;
In advance thou has taken the trail up to heaven
  To locate a camp for the rest of the boys.

TO CHARLEY.

MY DEAR OLD PARD.

LONELY to-night in my little log cabin,
  I am thinking of you and the days long ago,
When together we sat on the peak of old Harney,
  Drinking the grandeur of nature below.
True, it *was* grand, and well I remember
  The rapture that beamed in your bright sunny eyes
As you looked through the glass tow'rd the valley of Custer,
  With her thousands of peaks towering up to the skies.

Then did we picture the great Eastern cities,
  Comparing the grandeur of nature and art,
While you said—no art can compare with this picture ;
  And I acquiesced from the depths of my heart ;
For e'en when a boy I loved the wild mountains,
  The green, flowery valleys, the laughter of rills ;
And often in fancy and dreamland I wander
  Back to my boyhood among the wild hills.

My comrades, the brave pioneers of the mountains,
  Loved their young chieftain, and I loved him too ;
The reason was fully explained at your cabin,
  The day that I borrowed that bronco* from you.
And when we returned from the chase the next morning,
  Your welcoming shout and your honest embrace
Was more to me then than the laurels of glory,
  Won by the proudest of all Adam's race.

* Charley W. was the special correspondent of the Kansas City *Times* for the Black Hills. When Charley first made my acquaintance I was sitting astride of a half-cut log on my half-built cabin. We had many hunts together, and on one occasion the Indians got our whole camp outfit, together with my saddle, field-glasses, and my saddle bags, containing my scrap-book, which contained copies of scraps I had saved for over six years. One morning the Indians ran off with sixteen head of horses, and my white charger among the rest. I rushed down to Charley's tent, and he gave me his bronco to go after the reds. Twelve of our boys started, and we returned next day with eight of the stolen horses, which the Indians were forced to drop.

Oh, what a life—away from temptation—
   Away from the snares of life's busy throng,
Singing in chorus those odes of the woodland
   In notes that were tuned by the mocking-bird's song.
In ignorant bliss, and oh, how much better
   Than knowledge that's only acquired to deceive,
By hypocrites robbing the widow and orphan,
   And crimes that are almost too vile to believe.

And yet how I yearned for the knowledge you gave me,
   For you were the first who had taken my hand—
You were the first to encourage me onward,
   And picture my future in language most grand ;
And since then my verses, the fruit of my nature,
   These unpolished roughs, the impulse of my heart,
Have found some admirers e'en among critics
   Well versed in literature, science and art.

Thus while the bright star of hope is before me
   I still shall continue to work with a will ;
Determined to scale all the heights of misfortune,
   And slowly creep over adversity's hill.
Then, my dear friend, when the height of ambition
   Is mine—and way up on the summit I stand—
I shall think of the comrade who first gave me courage—
   Who gave me new life and a brother's right hand.

IN THE MOUNTAINS, February 28, 1879.

ODE TO CARIBOO FRIENDS.

AT last I must leave you, dear home in the mountains,
   At last say farewell to your dear Cariboo !
No longer to sip from its bright pearly fountains
   The cool draught of water distilled from the dew.
Oh, Barker, fair village, adown by the brook-side,
   Where millions have sprang from thy watery breast,
Fear not for thy future, fair queen of the mountains,
   For millions and millions are still 'neath each crest.

I feel it, believe it, God knows I speak truly,
   And would that some others might speak as they believe ;
But when experts grow zealous, Oh, Lord, how unruly !
   And in their excitement don't care to deceive.
But Time is a worker much better than experts,
   Though slowly, yet surely, he makes all things right ;
And so when some experts are dead and forgotten,
   Your dear Cariboo will be prosperous and bright.

Farewell, dear old comrades, you old Forty-niners,
   God bless you, dear boys, till I meet you again !
Which will be ere the snowflakes have covered your cabins,
   So sure as the sunshine which follows the rain.
Leave you forever ? How could you believe it—
   Leave all the home I have got in this world ?
No ! and returning I never *will* leave it
   Till justice is *done and the truth is unfurled.*

BARKERVILLE, B. C.

OUR "JACK."

IN MEMORIAM.

Lines written on the death of John Bilsland, who was killed by a slide of snow while attempting to get it off the shaft-house on Burns's Creek, Cariboo, March 13th, 1879.

AND still they go, the very best,
   Cut down in their youth and bloom.
There's something amiss in this region of ours,
I reckon we must have offended the powers,
For the Lord is culling our favorite flowers,
   And another is laid in the tomb ;
Another is laid 'neath the sod to rest—
   Killed before life had its noon.

I have seen, sometimes, on the battle field,
   The pride of our company fall,
But I never felt as I did that day
When they told me that Jack had passed away—

Jack, who was always happy and gay,
　　And one who would spend his all.
Prospecting deep, taking chances of yield,
　　He would stand with his boys or fall.

Escaping the perils of land and sea,
　　Unharmed for many a year,
And standing now by the shaft-house door,
As oft he stood in the days of yore ;
Then up the ladder, on roof once more,
　　A man who knew no fear.
Then down with the cruel snow went he—
　　No friend, no comrade near.

A good yet peculiar man was Jack,
　　And a thoroughbred mountaineer ;
No matter what hurt, he would never squeal—
His name was *honor*, and true as steel—
And his comrades say he could build a wheel
　　You could turn with a single tear ;
You smile—but I reckon I'm on the track,
　　Which to look at his work would appear.

One characteristic I want to note,
　　Though he had no child of his own,
How the children all to Jack would come
And say : " Uncle Jat, has oou dot some dum ?"
" No, but you bet I'll get you some."
　　And his eyes with rapture shone,
And voice like a chime of bells afloat,
　　With music in each tone.

The best mechanic without a doubt
　　(And I believe I can see it now),
Perhaps they have struck it rich up there ;
And hunting in vain, they could not scare
A man who could build a wheel to compare
　　With Jack. So, to show them how,
The angel of death put his light right out,
　　And I reckon he's there with them now.

All I can say, I must wish him well,
   If he's taken some heavenly stock,
For a prospect there on the heavenly shore
Is better than millions of gold in store.
And they say there are chances for millions more,
   Who can find (if they try) the bed rock—
That rock of ages, which yields so well,
   And Christ is the key to the lock.

UNDER THE SOD.

TO JOHN P.

Lines on the Death of Edwin L. Jones.

UNDER the sod he is sleeping to-day,
   Close by the sea-girdled shore ;
Under the sod and the dew and the clay,
   We can look on his face nevermore.
Jovial, kind-hearted, good-natured and free—
In peace let him sleep 'neath the shade of the tree
    In the land that he loved.

Under the sod they have laid him to rest,
   The lover of right and the hater of wrong ;
As honest a man as ever God blest,
   His love for a friend everlasting and strong.
And if for the wise and the good there is rest,
Then Edwin is surely at home with the blest,
    For the heavenly gates were ajar.

Under the sod near the murmuring sea,
   So far from the home of his childhood ;
So far from the cabin and old mountain tree,
   Where he sported with Sam in the wildwood.
His trials are over, his good deeds are done,
His battles are fought and the victory is won,
    And Edwin has gone to his God.

THE OLD MINER.

To the Boys of Cariboo.

I's a miner, I ar', an' a good un.
  It's nigh onto forty year
Since first I landed at 'Frisco,
  A youngster—with lots o' good cheer ;
I waltzed right inter the placer,
  An' struck it—you bet yer boots.
But I dropped it a-buckin' the tiger,
  Along with some other galoots.

But that didn't dampen my ardor.
  Ye see I war hearty an' strong,
An' I know'd by exertin' my muscle,
  I'd fetch it agin afore long ;
So back to the diggin's I travelled,
  But somehow about that time
There war heaps of the boys sick with fever,
  While I took ague in mine.

Wall, I thinned right down to a wafer,
  My clothes war too big for my chest,
I could made a respectable great-coat
  By jist tuckin' sleeves in my vest ;
But the diggin's war very onhealthy,
  An' so for a permanent cure
I struck for high ground on the mountains
  For pastures not greener, but newer.

Now here's where I *thought* that I struck it,
  This time it war quartz as I found,
An' so I kept pokin' an' gaddin'
  Till one day a stranger come round.
An' told me as how he war huntin'
  A permanent place to reside ;
An' so I sez, " Here ar' my fortin,
  And plenty for you, pard, beside."

He stayed with me two weeks, then wilted ;
  Said he, pard, I've bin thar afore ;
It 'tain't no use workin' for nothin',
  An' for grub we war nigh run ashore ;
So he left me ; an' bout a week after
  Another come joggin' along,
With plenty o' grub. So I sold out ;
  He bought me for—well, just a song.

Now I never did swar, 'tain't my nater,
  But, Lord ! when I heerd o' their game,
I reckin the air smelt o' brimstone—
  Wall, swarin' ar' too mild a name.
This rooster (who'd bin thar afore, mind)
  War an expert from 'Frisco, ye see ;
So he skinned out, and sent his stool pigeon
  To work that bonanza for me.

Since then I've been down on these experts,
  Like him as has been here with you ;
He comed like the rest do from 'Frisco,
  An' hark ye—condemned Cariboo.
Now, pards, I's an old veteran miner,
  My ha'rs have grown gray in the biz,
Don't go a cent on this expert,
  My 'pinion 'll stand agin his.

MY OWN MOUNTAIN TREE.

Written on the back of a photograph, under a palm tree, in Los Angeles, California.

UNDER a palm tree reclining,
  Away from the turmoil and strife,
The sun in his glory is shining—
  All nature seems grafted with life ;
The birds sing as sweetly above me,
  So happy are they in their glee ;
But give me the dear friends who love me,
  And birds on my own mountain tree.

MOTHER'S PRAYERS.

In the dreary hours of midnight,
    When the camp's asleep and still,
Not a sound, save rippling streamlets,
    Or the voice of the whippoorwill.
Then I think of dear, loved faces,
    As I steal around my beat—
Think of other scenes and places,
    And a mother's voice so sweet.

Mother, who, in days of childhood,
    Prayed as only mothers pray :
Guard his footsteps in the wild wood,
    Let him not be led astray ;
And when dangers hovered o'er me,
    When my life was full of cares,
Then a sweet form passed before me,
    And I thought of mother's prayers.

Mother's prayers ! Ah ! sacred memory,
    I can hear her sweet voice now,
As, upon her death-bed lying,
    With her hand upon my brow,
Calling on a Saviour's blessing,
    Ere she climbed the Golden Stairs.
There's a sting in all transgressing,
    When I think of mother's prayers.

And I made her one dear promise—
    Thank the Lord, I've kept it, too ;
Yes, I promised God and mother
    To the pledge I would be true.
Though a hundred times the tempter
    Every day throws out his snares,
I can boldly answer, "No, sir !"
    When I think of mother's prayers.

And while here, I tell the story
   Why my boyhood's days were sad ;
Is there not some one before me
   Who will make a mother glad?
Swell her heart with fond emotion—
   Drive away life's bitter cares ;
Sign and keep the pledge for mother—
   Heed thy mother's earnest prayers.

There is no one on the prairie
   Who must say it more than I—
No—I never drink. I thank you,
   I can never take your rye ;
And there's not in many hundreds
   Not a man who ever dares
Ask me drink when I have told him
   How I thought of mother's prayers.

Oh, my brother, do not drink it,
   Think of all your mother said ;
While upon her death-bed laying,
   Or perhaps she is not dead ;
Don't you kill her, then, I pray you,
   She has got enough of cares.
Sign the pledge, and God will help you,
   If you think of mother's prayers.

"CORPORAL BILL."

A CAMP in the mountains.   The pine-knot fire
Drove the gloomy shadows up higher and higher,
Till trees, and rocks, and the purling stream,
And the sun-tanned faces were all agleam
With the ruddy glow of the dancing light,
That shone like a gem in a setting of night.
Around the fire sat a picturesque group—
A small detail from a cavalry troop :

Bronzed old soldiers, who knew no fear,
Who had served as vets on that wild frontier ;
Who were used to the fray and the night alarms
From painted demons, who came in swarms.
Near by their horses were cropping the grass
That grew up wild in the mountain pass,
And near to the saddle-pillowed head
Of each grass-cushioned, blanketed bed
Lay carbines and pistols, near at hand,
In easy reach of the scouting band,
If the picket, who up on a cliff laid low,
Should give the alarm of a coming foe.
Around the camp fire the warrior throng
Enlivened the hours with story and song,
And merry laughter, borne out on the breeze,
Went rippling, echoing up through the trees.
Hark ! The sound of a horse's hoofs were heard
Coming up the gulch like a fleeting bird,
And the soldiers grasped their arms, and stood
With eager eyes peering into the wood.
From the sombre shadows came dashing out
A steaming horse and a buckskinned scout.
A scout from the fort ! The blue-clad men
Laid down their trusty rifles again,
And stood and waited with eager ear
The news from the busy world to hear.
The scout dismounted, and, bowing his head,
But four words whispered—"Boys, Grant is dead !"
There were trembling lips and pain-marked eyes,
And tears, and mutterings of surprise,
But not a word was spoken until,
In a trembling voice, old Corporal Bill
Cried out, "Jack, boy, don't say it is true !
Don't say it is taps—it may be tattoo !
Maybe he is waiting for orders to go—
But tell us – oh, tell us it is not so !
Grant dead ! Oh, no—come, come, old Jack,
Jes' say it's a joke, an' take it back !

Yes, please do, comrade –jes' crack a smile,
An' tell us you've galloped many a mile
To have a little fun with the boys,
An' check fur a while their camp-fire joys ;
Do this, ol' pard, an' we'll laugh an' sing
'Till the echo comes back with a merry ring !
Too true ? Ah ! yes ; I know by yer look
It's as true as the word in the holy book,
An' it cuts my heart like a knife ! Why, men,
I've fought under Grant again an' again ;
My ol' commander, back in the days
When the South with the flames o' war was ablaze.
I've followed him over many a field
Whar smoke-blackened columns quivered an' reeled
With the dreadful shock of an iron hail
That would make the face of the stoutest pale !
I have followed him through the lead-blazed wood
Whar the leaves war speckled with hero blood,
An' out over many a battle plain
Whar the ground war heaped with the warriors slain,
An' the piercin' rays o' the sun war broke
An' held in check by the clouds o' smoke
That poured from many an iron throat,
An' hung overhead, an' seemed to gloat,
Like black-faced demons, from realms of woe,
O'er the fearful carnage an' death below !
The upturned faces, in death so pale !
The dreadful song o' the leaden hail !
The quivering, mutilated flesh !
The piercin' yells o' the mad secesh !
The shriekin', howlin', screamin' shell !
Why, men, it must 'a-looked like hell,
With a million devils, in impish glee,
'Turned loose on a holiday jamboree !
An' right on the field, ridin' here an' there,
His horse a-sweatin' from every hair,
Rode Grant, as cool as a drippin' spring,
His keen eye watchin' the front an' wing,

A cigar half smoked in his teeth, his face
Bearin' stern resolution in every trace.
Wharever he rode the men would cheer,
Fur it nerved 'em to feel that he war near,
Fur they all knowed Grant, an' loved him, too,
An' the general loved his boys in blue.
An' now he is dead! The grand ol' chief
Has resigned his post to the last relief,
An' it chokes me up fur to think that he
Should be taken, an' such ol' cusses as me
Are left, sort o' useless, here below,
In the land that loved the general so.
Well, pards, it war God as took him away—
He musters the blue an' He musters the gray—
An' I reckon He needed that warrior grim
To serve as aid on the staff with Him—
An', comrades, who knows, in that better land,
But God may give him his old command?

THE VETERAN AND HIS GRANDSON.

Dedicated to Corporal James Tanner.

HOLD on! Hold on! My goodness, you take my breath, my son,
A-firin' questions at me, like shots from a Gatlin' gun—
Why do I wear this eagle an' flag an' brazen star,
An' why do my old eyes glisten when somebody mentions war?
Au' why do I call men " comrade," an' why do my eyes grow bright,
When you hear me tell your grandma I'm goin' to post to-night?
Come here, you inquisitive rascal, an' set on your grandpa's knee.
An' I'll try an' answer the broadsides you've been a-firin' at me.

Away back there in the sixties, and long afore you were born,
The news come a-flashin' to us, one bright an' sunny morn,

That some of our Southern brothers, a-thinkin', no doubt, 'twar right,
Had trailed their guns on our banner, an' opened a nasty fight.
The great big guns war a-boomin', an' the shot flyin' thick and fast,
An' troops all over the southland war rapidly bein' massed,
An' a thrill went through the nation, a fear that our glorious land
Might be split an' divided an' ruined by mistaken brothers' hand.

Lord ! but wa'n't there excitement, an' didn't the boys' eyes flash ?
An' didn't we curse our brothers fur bein' so foolish an' rash ?
An' didn't we raise the neighbors with loud an' continued cheers,
When Abe sent out a dockyment a-callin' fur volunteers ?
An' didn't we flock to the colors when the drums began to beat,
An' didn't we march with proud step along this village street ?
An' didn't the people cheer us when we got aboard the cars,
With the flag a-wavin' o'er us, and went away to the wars ?

I'll never forget your grandma as she stood outside o' the train,
Her face as white as a snowdrift, her tears a-fallin' like rain—
She stood there quiet an' deathlike, 'mid all o' the rush an' noise,
Fur the war war a takin' from her her husband an' three brave boys—
Bill, Charley, and little Tommy—just turned eighteen, but as true
An' gallant a little soldier as ever wore the blue.
It seemed almost like murder for to tear her poor heart so,
But your granddad *couldn't* stay, baby, an' the boys war determined to go.

The evenin' afore we started she called the boys to her side,
An' told 'em as how they war always their mother's joy an' pride,
An' though her soul was in torture, an' her poor heart bleedin' an' sore,
An' though she needed her darlings, their country needed 'em more.
She told 'em to do their duty wherever their feet might roam,
An' to never forget in battle their mother war prayin' at home,
An' if (an' the tears nigh choked her) they should fall in front o' the foe,
She'd go to her blessed Saviour an' ax Him to lighten the blow.

Bill lays an' awaits the summons 'neath Spottsylvania's sod,
An' on the field of Antietam Charley's spirit went back to God ;
An' Tommy, our baby Tommy, we buried one starlit night
Along with his fallen comrades, just after the Wilderness fight.
The lightnin' struck our family tree, an' stripped it of every limb,
A-leavin' only this bare old trunk, a-standin' alone an' grim.

My boy, that's why your grandma, when you kneel to the God you love,
Makes you ax Him to watch your uncles, an' make 'em happy above.

That's why you sometimes see her with tear-drops in her eyes ;
That's why you sometimes catch her a-tryin' to hide her sighs ;
That's why at our great reunions she looks so solemn an' sad ;
That's why her heart seems a-breakin' when the boys are so jolly an' glad ;
That's why you sometimes find her in the bedroom overhead,
Down on her knees a-prayin', with their pictures laid out on the bed ;
That's why the old-time brightness will light up her face no more,
Till she meets her hero warriors in the camp on the other shore.

An' when the great war was over, back came the veterans true,
With not one star a-missin' from that azure field of blue ;
An' the boys who on field o' battle had stood the fiery test
Formed posts o' the great Grand Army in the North, South, East, an' the West.
Fraternity, Charity, Loyalty, is the motto 'neath which they train—
Their object to care for the helpless, an' banish sorrow an' pain
From the homes o' the widows an' orphans o' the boys who have gone before,
To answer their names at roll-call in that great Grand Army Corps.

An' that's why we wear these badges, the eagle an' flag an' star,
Worn only by veteran heroes who fought in that bloody war ;
An' that's why my old eyes glisten while talkin' about the fray,
An' that's why I call men "comrade" when I meet 'em every day ;
An' that's why I tell your grandma, "I'm goin' to post to-night,"
For there's where I meet the old boys who stood with me in the fight,
And, my child, that's why I've taught you to love an' revere the men
Who come here a-wearin' badges to fight those battles again.

They are the gallant heroes who stood 'mid the shot an' shell,
An' follered the flyin' colors right into the mouth o' hell—
They are the men whose valor saved the land from disgrace an' shame,
An' lifted her back in triumph to her perch on the dome o' fame ;
An' as long as you live, my darling, till your pale lips in death are mute,
When you see that badge on a bosom, take off your hat an' salute ;
An' if any ol' vet should halt you, an' question why you do,
Just tell him you've got a right to, fur your granddad's a comrade too.

LILLIE.

"Last evening, at the Bush Street Theatre, a beautiful incident occurred, not down on the bills, however, yet which was highly appreciated by the large audience present. It is well known that Captain Jack Crawford, the hardy mountaineer, scout, poet, and actor, has an especial predilection for children, and he is in the zenith of his joy when he has a bevy of them around him, spinning his extravagant stories, and otherwise amusing them. Last evening the captain was sitting in the orchestra circle, when he was espied by a four-year-old flaxen-haired beauty across the theatre. Quick as thought she left her mother's side, ran clear around the circle, and without the slightest ceremony seated herself on the captain's lap, not only to his surprise, but, from appearances, to his delight, for he entertained the little 'waif' the balance of the evening. The incident was a very pleasing one."—*San Francisco Footlight.*

SHE left her loving mother's side
    And climbed upon my knee—
A lovely little blue-eyed child,
    Who spoke her love for me.
I gazed upon the throng around,
    On fashion's daughters fair,
But not one tress in all that throng
    Could match sweet Lillie's hair.

God bless her! Just a little while
    I held her to my breast;
Forgetting all life's cares at once,
    I waited her request.
And then in whispers soft and low,
    And pointing over there,
Said she, " My mamma told me once
    That oou had till'd a bear."

I never saw the play—not I
    Indeed—I did not care,
For I was happy spinning yarns
    For little golden-hair;
And how her little blue eyes shone
    Each time a story ended,
And how she almost shouted out,
    " Oh my, but dat was sp'endid !"

" Oh, dear ! and must we really do ?
   I wish it wasn't out ;
I feel so very dood,
   I wish dat I tood shout."
Sweet angel ! you have brought me joy,
   And filled me with delight ;
May angels guard you all through life—
   God bless you, child, good-night !

MY BIRTHDAY.

My birthday ! yet 'twas accidental
   That I found it came to-day ;
Lonely in my cabin musing,
   How the time does pass away—
Not a soul to wish me gladness,
   Not a friend to pull my ears ;
While my heart is filled with sadness,
   Thinking of the passing years.

Once I had an angel mother—
   How she used to bring me joy ! .
Birthdays one upon the other,
   I was still her favorite boy.
But the angels took her from me —
   Dead and gone these many years—
She who was my guardian angel
   In this thorny vale of tears.

How she used to pray, " God bless him !"
   While the tear-drops filled her eyes,
With a mother's tender pleading,
   Looking upward toward the skies.
Oh, my mother ! if thy spirit
   Hovers near me while alone,
Bless once more thy wayward offspring
   In this little cabin home.

IN THE MOUNTAINS, CARIBOO, March 4.

(Taken from "Tic Tacs," by permission of Homer Lee Bank-Note Co.)

LITTLE REVILEE.

I HAIN'T much love fur an Injun,
　Take Injuns as they go,
An' for many a year on this wild frontier,
　I've been their bitterest foe ;
An' I reckon as you uns know me,
　An' I ain't much given to boast,
But listen to me--I wouldn't be
　Unjust to an Injun's ghost.

So jest let up on that redskin,
　At least fur a minute or two,
An' I'll tell you why he ain't goin' to die,
　If you b'lieve w'at I say is true.

Let me attend to his talkin',
    Fur you see he is off'n the track,
An' I'll try to tell how he went through hell,
    With me but a kid on his back.

Make no mistake ; I know him,
    But I reckon he don't know me—
Leastwise he don't know I'm little Joe,
    As they called Little Revilee ;
But, pards, can't you all remember,
    When only a little kid,
Some kind word said by a friend now dead,
    That remains in your heart deep hid ?

Wal, so it was with Scar Face—
    That ugly one-eyed red,
An' you all kin bet I won't forget
    Till gratitude is dead.
That uncouth face was handsome
    That morn in Fifty-three,
When mother lay dead an' father had fled
    From his Little Revilee.

They had sent me fur ammunition,
    Just after the reds had struck —
'Twas a desperate trip, but I had to skip—
    Fur a kid I had lots o' pluck ;
An' I lost no time in reachin'
    The camp, ten miles away.
But when I got back to our little shack
    I had a lone hand to play.

Thar' lay my father an' mother,
    An' as over their bodies I stood
An' Injun came an' called me his game,
    But I made him w'at we calls good.
Then a dozen more came on me,
    An' with mother's head on my knee,
I fired my last shot—then all was a blot
    To Little Revilee.

When I cum to myself an Injun
   War bathin' my achin' head,
While all around, piled up on the ground,
   Laid the hostiles thick an' dead,
While the one with me war a-bleedin',
   His face hacked up with knives—
In the dreadful strife he had saved my life
   At the cost o' a dozen lives.

Now, I hain't much love fur an Injun,
   Take Injuns as they go ;
But angels fell to a place called hell,
   An' thar's angels here below.
An' look ye, boys, that's the Injun
   As kept the red niggers from me,
An' you hear me toot, if he hangs I shoot,
   Fur I'm still Little Revilee.

You hain't got nuthin' agin him
   But prowlin' around the camp,
So you all made a lope for a lariat rope
   To hang him right up for a scamp.
But I say he's goin' to travel
   Safe out o' this chapparel,
An' the very fust one makes a play with a gun,
   Will land in a minute in hell.

DECORATION DAY.

COMRADES, our nation is thinking to-day
   Of her glorious salvation, and counting the cost
Of the men who are sleeping beneath the cold clay—
   The noble, the gallant, and brave that we lost—
That we lost ! Yet how fondly we cherish their names—
   How eager to tell of the deeds they have done,
Their actions so brave, that their glory and fame
   Are pictured and told in the battles they won !

Let our nation rejoice, then, 'mid sorrow to-day—
  Let our hearts beat with love for the flag of the free ;
While the widows and orphans are kneeling to pray,
  Great God of the Universe, humbly to Thee,
And we who have safely returned from the fight,
  Would ask Thee, most humbly, dear Father, again
To watch o'er our actions, that we, by Thy might,
  May show that our comrades have not died in vain.

Dear comrades, the widow has come ; stand aside—
  Let her kneel by the tomb, unresponsive forever,
Where moulders the arm of the true and the tried:
  Her guard and protector, till war bid them sever.
Stand aside, boys, she comes, as she's come all these years,
With a wreath, lovely wreath, all bespangled with tears,
And a prayer, Heavenly Father, when this life is done,
Reunite us in heaven with loved Washington.

The orphan has come, boys ; let him have a place
To look at the orator straight in the face,
To listen once more, hear recounted the story,
For his sire was a soldier, and shared in the glory ;
And he, too, has vowed, on each thirtieth of May,
His love for our Union ; God bless him ! we say.

The patriot is here and the statesman has come,
The actor, the student, yea, every one ;
The dwellers in palace, and hovel so plain—
All—all have done honor to the slain.
Let the blossoms of May bow their heads o'er each grave,
And breathe balms of sweetness all over the brave,
And lilies, pure lilies, with roses so red,
Be strewn with a wreath on the graves of the dead ;
While tears of the widows and orphans like dew
Are mingled with flow'rets of red, white, and blue.

And now as these heroes lie sleeping beneath
The Stars and the Stripes, the flowers and the wreath,

We think of the trenches dug after the fight,
When wrapt in their blankets at dead of the night,
We buried in hundreds, yea, thousands, the brave,
Embracing each other; no mark o'er their grave,
Save that simple inscription, one word alone,
You read it with awe, and pronounce it "Unknown."
And to-day of the four hundred thousand who fell,
The wife, and the mother, and sister, will tell,
Oh, how generous, how loyal, how noble and true,
They died for our Union, for me and for you!

Our Union still lives.   They have not died in vain,
And to-day we've adorned their graves once again;
But those flowers, and the hands that have strewn them to-day,
In death will soon languish, and all pass away.
And these monuments, too, so majestic and grand,
Will crumble to dust.   Yet our Union will stand—
And that is their monument, ours, too, as well,
Who fought by the side of the noble who fell;
Who suffered in cabin, in camp, and in field,
And swore by yon flag that we never would yield
Till that flag, lovely flag, dearest flag of the free,
Should float, boys, in triumph, for you and for me.

And here as we gather to-day 'neath its stars,
And look upon comrades with crutches and scars,
And sleeves, empty sleeves, hanging loose by their side,
The boys who survived 'mid the thousands who died—
And yet do they murmur? No, no! nor complain.
"Each man owes a part," say the wounded and maim,
"And we have but acted our part in the strife,
And gave but a limb, while the dead gave their life."
Oh, comrades, how hallowed the ground where they sleep—
Where the widows and orphans are kneeling to weep
O'er the brave who have fallen in skirmish and fight,
Protecting that flag and the cause that was right!

And yet we have still a great duty to do—
Work on, loyal hearts, until death's last tattoo

Shall lull us to rest 'neath the flag of the free,
Till awakened by angels, a sweet reveille,
From the boys who have gone, and whose marching is o'er,
They are watching on picket, on Canaan's bright shore.

OUR MARTYRED DEAD.

GENERAL E. D. BAKER.

The following poem was read by me at the tomb of General E. D. Baker, on
Decoration Day, 1879. The three first verses are mine; those following by
M. P. Griffis, General E. D. Baker Post, Philadelphia.

SOLDIERS, comrades, gather round me,
    List the story I will tell
Of a noble, gallant soldier—
    One who loved our flag so well.
Here he sleeps beneath the daisies,
    Here, beneath the mossy sod,
Near the broad Pacific's murmur,
    He is mouldering with the clod.

Oh, how brave—methinks I see him'
    Charging—leading, sword in hand,
With the courage of our Custer,
    At the head of his command.
Onward! upward! rally! comrades,
    See! the rebels giving way!
Ah! Ball's Bluff, you had a martyr
    When our Baker fell that day.

While we gather round his ashes,
    Comrades far beyond the plain
Send a tribute to his mem'ry
    From the Post that bears his name.
Baker Post, in Philadelphia—
    Boys who joined him in the fray—
Bade me tell you how they loved him,
    And I speak for them to-day.

IN MEMORIAM.

Eighteen years have passed, dear comrades,
  Since the man whose name we bear
Bade farewell to rank and station,
  But a soldier's lot to share—
Onward marching with the army—
  Onward fighting for the free—
By a pure and holy purpose
  He was guided to the sea.

Oh, my comrades, over yonder,
  In the far Pacific State,
Sleeps our brave commander, Baker,
  Close beside the Golden Gate.
Heaven's dew will wet the laurels,
  Comrades' hands will strew sweet flowers,
Some brave boy will read this tribute
  O'er that martyred brave of ours.

Tell the friends who gather round you
  How he fought to gain the day ;
How, when cruel death had marked him,
  Faint and bleeding in the fray.
Tell them, comrades, how, when dying,
  "Charge !" he said : "Boys, take the hill !
Yes, thank God ! I see it waving !
  See ! our flag is floating still !"

Thus he died a gallant hero,
  Soldier, statesman—none more grand.
Strew his grave with sweetest flowers,
  Comrades of the sunny land.
And when death has claimed our army,
  When life's pilgrimage is o'er,
May we meet our martyred Baker,
  Now at peace for evermore.

OFF TO THE PICNIC.

To ye Sons o' Caledonia.

Awa', ye brawny sons o' Scotland !
  Up the banks and doon the braes,
Through the Hielands o' Nevada,
  Sing yo'r songs o' ither days ;
Yet it's no rich gowrey's valley,
  Nor the Forth's dear sunny side ;
Nor the wild and mossy mountain,
  Father of the placid Clyde.

Yet just for the while imagine
  Ye are back on Scotia's shore,
'Mang the braes and grouse and heather
  Where the Highland waters roar ;
'Mang the groves o' sweetest myrtle,
  Or perhaps aside the Doon,
Thinking o' young Bobbie's courtship
  By the light o' bonnie moon.

Noble, brave, unselfish poet !
  Don't forget him 'mid yo'r joys ;
Fill and drink to him a bumper—
  He was nature's bard, my boys.
One o' Scotland's noblest freemen,
  Spurning lords and lairds and crown !
Here's to Scotia's bard and poet—
  Bobbie Burns—boys, drink her down.

Up in Heaven wi' Highland Mary,
  Burns now sings a sweeter song ;
He is wearing brighter laurels
  Than the men who did him wrong.
" Scots wha hae," methinks I hear it—
  " Bonnie Doon," ah ! how sublime ;
At yo'r picnic drink this bumper—
  " Bobbie Burns and Auld Lang Syne !"

GOLD HILL, NEV.

CATO'S IDEAS

ON THE NEW CHURCH DOCTRINE.

I WENT to church last Sunday,
　Which I allers want to do,
To hea' dat same old story,
　But I hea' ub sumfin new ;
An', wife, old Deacon Johnson,
　Who allers preached so well,
Come out an' tol' us darkeys
　Dar wasn't any hell.

Wharfor' he tol' dat story
　Is sumfin I don't know,
Kase if dar ain't no debil,
　Whar will dem wicked go ?
Kase 'tain't no use in preachin'
　If Adam nebber fell,
An' 'tain't no use in prayin'
　If cussin' does as well.

Now, dis chile ain't no angel,
　But you hea' Cato talk—
Dar's sumfin gwine to happen
　If 'gainst de Lord we balk ;
Kase if der was no 'Mighty,
　Dat sun he nebber shine,
An' you jest bet sich preachin'
　Ain't gwine to win dis time.

I can't jest understan' it,
　Kase jest two weeks ago
He tol' us how ole Satan
　Was roamin' to an' fro ;
An' now dar ain't no debil,
　An' no sich place of fire ;
Dis chile don't take no chances—
　I's gwine to clim' up higher.

MY HERO.

My Hero! The wealth of the world could not purchase the noble fellow. He is a grand specimen of the Albino St. Bernard, white as the driven snow, with large hazel eyes that beam with almost human intelligence, and he weighs one hundred and forty-seven pounds. But for his love and devotion my body would to-day be buried in the treacherous quicksand over which the Rio Grande flows on its ceaseless journey to the sea. Captain S. C. Plummer, of the regular army, witnessed my rescue by my noble Hero, and telegraphed the following account of it to the Denver *Tribune:*

"Last Monday a number of soldiers went from Fort Craig to the Rio Grande for a bath. Among them was Captain Jack Crawford. After being in the water about three quarters of an hour Captain Jack started to cross toward the other side over a sand-bar, on which the water was only from six inches to a foot deep. Several of the others followed Jack, and they had considerable fun, tripping each other and rolling over in the water, while two of the boys got Jack down in the shallow water and tickled him in the ribs until he was nearly exhausted with laughter, he being very ticklish. In order to get away from his tormentors, Jack rolled over toward the deep water at the edge of the bar, and when he got upon his feet he kept backing down stream, and although there was not over two feet of water where he stood, yet the current was so strong that it would carry him down should he lose his footing. He kept splashing water on those who had been tickling him, and bantering them to come on after him, when suddenly he made two or three desperate efforts to get back, but failed. Yet he said not a word, or the others might have joined hands and reached him. No one dreamed for a moment that he was trying to extricate himself from the quicksand. All at once he went down like a piece of lead. Even then we thought he had taken a dive, until he was under water longer than a man would willingly stay, and, indeed, no one would have noticed this particularly, had we not heard a peculiar sound, more like the roar of a lion than anything else, and the next instant Jack's dog Hero, a beautiful St. Bernard, was seen swimming toward his master, while he set up a howl that seemed to say, 'I'm coming.' Jack came up about twenty-five yards below where he went down, and right in the centre of a terribly swift current, near where the river would make a quick, sharp turn. He was nearly exhausted when the sand broke from under him, and, striking a whirlpool, he could make little or no headway, and had to use all his strength to keep from being caught in the suction. Hill, a soldier, orderly for General Hatch, soon as he saw the dog go for Jack, also sprang in the current, but Hero got to Jack first, just as he was going down a second time, and taking him by the hair of the head, brought him above water. Jack, who never lost his presence of mind, caught the dog by the back, just above the hip, and the faithful Hero brought him safe to shore, nearly a mile below where he first went down. This was really a narrow escape, as an officer and five soldiers went down nearly in the same place a few years ago, and were never seen. A wagon and team of mules disappeared in the river a year ago, and have not turned up yet."

Can you wonder that I love my dog—my noble, faithful Hero? Can you wonder that I hold him above all price—that the riches of the world could not induce me to part with him? But a few months since a New York millionaire was at my ranch at Fort Craig, New Mexico, and asked me to fix a price on the dog, and in response I wrote for him the following poem :

HERO.

To my Friend H. K.

WHAT'LL I take fur that handsome dorg?
　Wal, mister, how much are you worth?
A million! Ge whiz! That's a heap o' scads.
　Wal, I ain't got a dollar on airth,
An' I reckon as how ye'll believe me, pard,
　When I tell you I never struck ile ;
But Hero's a great big bonanza to me,
　An' he couldn't be bought fur yer pile.

Wal, no, he's never been trained, 'cause you see
　He's a kind of a self-made dog,
An' even when only a bit of a purp
　He wouldn't be seen with a hog.
An' he jest grow'd up with our blue-eyed May,
　An' they sported out thar on the lee,
An' one day I found 'hat the noble ol' boy
　Had a load of affection fur me.

An' you'd like the story? Wal, 'tain't very long—
　Jest look at them big, honest eyes ;
He knows as how I'm talkin' 'bout him,
　An' that's why he's lookin' so wise,

'Cause he knows purty much every word as I say—
  He's corralled as much sense as some men—
An', pard, if I hadn't a squar meal on earth,
  He wouldn't go back on me then.

No, friendship like that you don't see every day—
  It's as pure as the daisies that grow;
My Hero has no selfish motives, except
  He expects all the love I bestow;
An' if through misfortune the wolf hangs around,
  Or if sickness should knock at my door,
You can bet yer whole pile he will stay at my side,
  Fur he's faithful an' true to the core.

But why do I love him? Wal, now, let me see—
  It war just about five year ago,
I war caught in an eddy—the old Rio Grande,
  If she clutches you, ha'es to let go.
Wal, Hero jest lay on the bank over thar,
  An' when others war deaf to my call
My Hero cum to me, an' why I'm alive
  Is jest 'cause he saved me, that's all.

An' I reckon as how you will pardon me, sir,
  If I tell you that gold cannot buy
The friend as has proved himself loyal to me,
  Since I've told you the wherefore an' why;
Fur even a dog has a heart, don't ye know,
  An' sometimes it's loyal an' true;
An' somehow I think, when I look in his eyes,
  As thar' must be a dog-heaven, too.

When I return to my home Hero will be the first to bound down the Rio Grande hill to meet and welcome me with a joyful bark—a bark that will notify the loved ones up in the ranch that I am again at home. His noble white head will be the first to receive my caresses after my absence, and his will be the first lovelit eyes to look into mine with touching eloquence. He will lead me with joyful bounds up the hill to wife and children—up to the door of my humble but cherished home on the banks of the old Rio Grande.

THE GRAVE OF MY MOTHER.

A SONG.

To Mrs. Emily Pitt Stevens, San Francisco.

There's a green grassy mound in the valley I love,
  Where angels their vigils are keeping ;
The pine trees are singing a dirge far above,
  The sky pearly tear drops is weeping,
And cooing on high is a bright turtle dove
  O'er the grave where my mother is sleeping.

Chorus.

  Peacefully sleeping, she sleeps 'neath the clay,
    This world cannot give me another ;
  No one to guide me, and no one to pray,
    While I weep o'er the grave of my mother.

The dew-drops are falling, the evening is here,
  And o'er me night's shadows are stealing ;
All nature is silent, good angels are near,
  And hushed is the harvester's reaping,
While fondly I linger 'mid memories dear,
  Near the grave where my mother is sleeping.

Chorus.

Oh, here let me linger in silence and bliss,
  While only the starlets are peeping,
And mix with the dewdrops a tear and a kiss,
  O'er the grave where my mother is sleeping ;
For no spot on earth is so sacred as this—
  This spot where my dear mother's sleeping.

Chorus.

NORA LEE.

A SONG.

I HAVE watched the roses blooming
  And the violets' lovely hue,
And daisies like the starlight
  As they sparkled with the dew ;
I have looked upon the lilies
  And the flowers of every tree,
But none were half so pretty
  As my blue-eyed Nora Lee.

Chorus.

  She is sweeter than the violets,
    She is fairer than the rose ;
  Her eyes are soft and tender,
    And her cheek with beauty glows.
  Oh, I never can forget her,
    Though she never thinks of me ;
  I love that blue-eyed beauty—
    Little darling, Nora Lee.

To my prairie home I'm going,
  With my comrades brave and free,
And yet where'er I wander
  Those blue eyes will follow me.
I shall see them in the camp fire,
  They will sparkle in the dell,
And in the rippling streamlets
  I shall hear that last farewell.
                  Chorus.

God bless you, Jack ! God bless you !
  Were the words she whispered low ;
I thought 'twas heavenly music
  From her throat as white as snow.

And my heart beat in a tremor,
  So she spake kind words to me.
I wish I did not love her —
  Darling, blue-eyed Nora Lee.

                    Chorus.

I have gazed upon the streamlets
  When the moon was shining bright,
The rippling of the waters
  In the summer noon of night.
I have looked on nature's grandeur,
  On the prairie, land, and sea,
But none of them could charm me
  Like the voice of Nora Lee.

                    Chorus.

Oh, no matter where I wander,
  Her sweet image will be there ;
Her blue eyes shine upon me,
  And her voice be everywhere.
And though I pine in sorrow,
  She is all the world to me ;
May angels guard my fairy—
  Darling, blue-eyed Nora Lee !

                    Chorus.

OUR FIRST REUNION AND CAMP-FIRE.

Respectfully dedicated to F. B. Gowan, brother of my brave colonel, who fell while leading us in storming the rebel post at Petersburg, April 2d, 1865.

With love—which time can never change—
  We grasp each other's hands,
And think of battles fought and won—
  Of Burnside's stern commands ;
Bright memories of the hallowed past
  Are stealing through our souls,
While thinking of the noble dead
  Now mustered from our rolls.

At times our hearts would almost bleed,
  And angels seemed to frown ;
But God was on the ramparts, boys,
  While the mortars tumbled down ;
And though at times a boy was hit
  With a fragment of a shell,
We stood it—did we not, comrades?
  In the ramparts of Fort Hell.

And when we went on picket,
  With our blankets on our arm,
And each a stick of wood, comrades,
  To try and keep us warm ;
How oft we thought of happy homes,
  Of friends and parents, too,
And lovely little blue-eyed girls
  Who'd die for me and you !

And often, when we shouted
  Across to Johnny Reb,
To throw us some tobacco,
  And we would throw them bread,
How quickly they responded !
  And the plugs came thick and fast,
And we shared them with each other—
  And shared them to the last.

But though they gave tobacco,
  And though we gave them bread,
Between the lines we soon must see
  The dying and the dead !
And though Mahone defied us,
  And though her strength was great,
Who would dare to charge them, boys,
  If not our Forty-eight ?

And when our greatest generals
  Defied our boys alone,
To charge the enemy in front
  And capture Fort Mahone—

Oh, can you e'er forget it, boys?
  The answer Gowan sent :
" We'll take it, with the help of God,
  Or die in the attempt !"

And nobly on that fatal day
  He led us on so well,
Till fairly on their ramparts, boys,
  Our noble colonel fell.
And did you mark the change, comrades?
  Where was the leader now
Who dared to lead us on like he
  Who fell with shattered brow ?

I need not speak of others' deeds
  Who led us on before—
Of Nagle and of Siegfried, too,
  Brave Pleasants and Gilmore.
Oh, no ! their names are written
  On a grateful nation's shrine,
And nothing can erase them, boys,
  Until the end of time.

Another word—each comrade's heart
  Is filled with gratitude
To Siegfried, Pleasants, Bosbyshell,
  Who were so kind and good
To offer us a banquet, boys,
  Such as we never saw—
Much better than the hard-tack, boys—
  Hurrah ! then, boys, hurrah !

But don't forget, another year
  Will soon pass o'er our head,
And then we hope to meet again—
  If living ; but, if dead,
May we not meet in heaven, boys,
  And see upon the shore
A picket guard of angels
  With Gowan and Gilmore ?

THE RANGERS' RETREAT.

A SONG.

'Tis a dear little spot in the valley I love,
    And the pine trees are waving above it ;
The home of the lark, the blackbird and dove—
    I never can tell how I love it.
I've roamed through its grandeur with rifle in hand,
    O'er beautiful streamlets and fountains ;
From Calamity Bar the scene was most grand,
    With its moss-covered rocks and its mountains.

Chorus.
    'Tis cosy, 'tis cheerful, that moss-covered dell—
    That dear little Eden where I used to dwell ;
    The flowers when in bloom cast a fragrance so sweet
    Through that dear little valley, the Rangers' Retreat.

Oh, 'tis speckled with daisies and covered with dew ;
    There's no spot so dear as that valley,
Where brothers met brothers, the brave and the true,
    And in danger 'round each other rally.
The deer and the antelope roam in the dell,
    The mocking-bird sings in the bushes,
While under the daisies the jack-rabbits dwell,
    And the water-snipe hides in the rushes. *Chorus.*

And, though I'm far from that valley to-day,
    The scenes are all pictured before me :
The deer are at water, the birds are at play,
    And the skylarks are all singing o'er me.
I think I can see my dear comrades of old,
    The sound of each rifle seems ringing ;
The echo comes back from that valley of gold,
    While the boys round the camp-fires are singing. *Chorus.*

THE POOR MAN'S SOLILOQUY.

AFTER POE.

To the Toiling Millions.

ONCE, when I was weak and weary,
And the day was cold and dreary,
I was famished, almost starving —
  Ragged were the clothes I wore,
I was thinking of suspensions,
And the railroad king's intentions,
For they were then in convention,
  Planning as they planned before ;
'Tis monopoly, I whispered,
  And the wolf is at our door —
  This it is   and nothing more.

Thus for hours I sat and pondered,
Sat and closed my eyes and wondered —
Wondered why these men of millions
  Were not like the men of yore ;
But the answer came — 'tis fashion,
Hoarding gold to please their passion,
With fancy teams forever dashing —
  Dashing past the poor man's door ;
Scornfully they look and mutter,
  As they pass the poor man's door :
  " Our slaves — and nothing more."

Your slaves ?   Aye, chained and fettered,
" Slave" on every brow is lettered ;
You will sign to our conditions,
  Or we'll grind you to the floor ;
You have, with a weak subjection,
Severed every free connection.
U. S. troops are our protection ;
  You have signed your names — ye swore
  To obey — and nothing more.

Oh, ye gods! And must we languish,
In our poverty and anguish?
Starve while money kings are planning
    How to keep their gold in store?
Is our country not enlightened,
Or its heads like cowards frightened,
That the reins should not be tightened
    On these robbers of the poor?
Yes! The toiling mass can do it!—
    We have changed such things before;
    Give them power—never more.

While corruption reigns in office,
Every knave and fool and novice,
For a sum of filthy lucre
    Will betray his trust—and more:
They will legislate to press you,
And in every way distress you;
Yet they'll meet you and caress you,
    But they're traitors to the core.
They will swear by all that's holy—
    For your vote—but nothing more.

Look toward the broad Atlantic,
See a million starving, frantic—
Bread or blood is what they're asking—
    Blood or bread to feed the poor,
Begging bread for which they're slaving—
Dangers on the railroad braving,
Want and hunger ever craving,
    Gnawing deep into the core,
While the railroad gods are basking
    On the Long Branch sunny shore:
    These are facts—and nothing more.

Must we beg to be in fetters?
Are these railroad kings our betters,
That we must like slaves approach them,
    While our wants they still ignore?

No! There must be some reaction ;
Something done to crush this faction—
Labor must have satisfaction,
   Though grim death stood at our door.
Shall I tell you how to get it—
   How to strike corruption's core ?
   Vote for tricksters—never more.

Oh, ye sons of toil and danger,
Christ was cradled in a manger—
He was poor and weak and lowly,
   Yet for us the cross He bore ;
But the rich-robed fiends they tried Him,
Persecuted and denied Him,
And with robbers crucified Him,
   Just for being Christ—and poor ;
Just because he killed corruption,
   Jesus died—and nothing more.

Can such beings ask for pardon,
While their hearts they ever harden ?
Can they ask for peace from Heaven,
   While its laws they still ignore ?
No, by all the hosts above us—
By the broken hearts that love us—
By the tears of many millions
   Of the wronged, down-trodden poor—
They can never reach that heaven
   Until hell is frozen o'er,
Which the Reverend Mr. Moody
   Tells us will be—never more.

THE FIRST FLOWER OF MAY.

In May, 1876, a band of Sioux drove off fourteen head of our horses, and after two days' chase we regained seven of them ; but, owing to the Indians having a change of horses, we failed to secure any scalps.   On the first evening, after a hard day's ride, we camped in a pleasant valley near a cooling spring of water. Frank Smith (Antelope Frank, as we called him) and myself had ridden about three miles further, in hopes of getting a sight of the Indian camp, and it was on our return to the valley mentioned above, and a venison supper, that we laid down to rest under a spreading pine, when the incidents occurred which called forth the following verses.

A DAISY ! the first I had seen in the spring,
  . Was peeping from under the sod ;
The air was so chilly, the wind was so cold,
    That I fear'd the fair daisy had made rather bold
To ascend from the earth's warmer clod.
    Just then a fair skylark flew heavenward to sing
Sweet anthems, in praise to his God.

How sweet to the traveller those soul-stirring notes,
    When weary with riding all day !
Indeed, it was joy to my comrade and me—
    The lark in the sky, and the flower on the lea,
And our weariness soon passed away,
    That night 'round the camp-fire we tuned up our throats
And sang of the first flower of May.

DEAR reader, farewell, the affliction is o'er—
  Your powers of endurance astound me ;
With my horse I am off for the trail once more,
  Where the wandering muse first found me.

www.ingramcontent.com/pod-product-compliance
Lightning Source LLC
Chambersburg PA
CBHW030607040726
47497CB00008B/2884